"As a mother of multiple children with serious health conditions, there are times when I don't know how or what to pray. Eric and Jessika's heartfelt, Scripture-based prayers put words to thoughts and feelings that can be hard to express, while also helping parents like me to look to God and hope in him."

Katie Faris, Author, *God Is Still Good* **and** *He Will Be Enough*

"As someone who has walked through multiple miscarriages, I can personally attest to the experience of deeply longing to cry out to the Lord yet having no words to do so. Eric and Jessika have given me those words. *In His Hands* gives simple yet profound examples of how and what to pray amidst loss, fear, or grief during a child's medical crisis, as well as the myriad of circumstances that come with it. This book is a gift to those who are walking through this season as well as those who are walking with them. Highly recommended!"

Kristin L. Kellen, Assistant Professor of Biblical Counseling, Southeastern Baptist Theological Seminary

"*In His Hands* is a precious resource for families who are clinging to God during the heartache and confusion of medical crises. These prayers are steeped in Scripture; they are full of humble wisdom, honest lament, and godly hope. When circumstances are so overwhelming that you don't even know what to say, these prayers will draw you close to God and help you find your voice."

Scott James, MD, Author, *When Your Child is Ill: Nurturing Faith in Hard Times*

"What a gift Schumacher and Sanders offer the hurting with *In His Hands*, a beautiful, poignant collection of prayers for those touched by child illness and loss. Nuanced with the wisdom of personal experience and saturated with Scripture, this book will offer a voice to the suffering when words fail, and point them to the one, true Word who has borne their sorrows and is acquainted with grief."

Kathryn Butler, MD, Author, *Between Life and Death* **and** *Glimmers of Grace*

"This beautiful book is deeply moving—the prayers are affective, touching the heart in a way that child, sibling, parents, and family will identify with. It is deeply pastoral—the prayers are comprehensive, covering all possible scenarios that child, sibling, parents, and family may experience. And it is deeply needed—the prayers are instructive, giving child, sibling, parents, and family words to pray when they know not how to pray. What a beautiful blessing this book will be to many!"

Jonathan Gibson, Author, *The Moon Is Always Round*

"This is a book for the moments when you don't have the words to pray. Eric and Jessika remind parents of the hope of the gospel with every prayer."

Kristin Schmucker, The Daily Grace Co.

"When our child faces a medical crisis, fears can paralyze, emotions can disorient, and we often lack the words to express the whirlpool of thoughts and feelings within. I was deeply impacted by these beautifully real prayers, which in many ways speak into countless circumstances. When you lack the words to pray, open the pages of this book and you will find the words your heart longs to cry out to your Heavenly Father."

Sarah Walton, Co-Author, *Together through the Storms*

"This book is a gift. It's not just a gift because you can (and should) gift it to suffering parents. It's a gift because it is written by people who have learned, through deep pain, how to suffer in faith. Rather than offering superficial platitudes, this little book will draw your heart deep into the heart of the Suffering Servant who knows and loves. I highly recommend it."

Elyse Fitzpatrick, Author, *Unloved: The Rejected Saints God Calls Beloved*

"By masterfully integrating the words of Scripture to help parents and children give voice to their laments, hopes, pleas and praises, this book helps us all to see how God meets us wherever we are in the pediatric medical crisis journey. Schumacher and Sanders offer these prayers as parents intimately familiar with crisis, and intimately familiar with the Lord who carries us through both healing and loss. This book is a much-needed resource for families walking through the indescribable tension between grief and hope, and for those looking to support loved ones in medical crisis with truthful, gritty, platitude-free faith."

Hui-wen (Alina) Sato, Pediatric ICU Nurse

"Using Scripture and compassion, *In His Hands* provides words and prayers for not only families facing difficult diagnoses but also those praying for them and their medical team. Today, I learned of a friend's cancer diagnosis and found comfort in this new resource. I plan to use it with our center staff and give it as a gift to families we support."

Michelle Nietert, MA, LPC-S, Clinical Director, HopeHelps.me

In His Hands

Eric M. Schumacher
and Jessika Sanders

In His Hands
© Eric M. Schumacher and Jessika Sanders, 2024

Published by:
The Good Book Company

thegoodbook.com | thegoodbook.co.uk
thegoodbook.com.au | thegoodbook.co.nz | thegoodbook.co.in

ISBN: 9781784989781 | JOB: 007663 | Printed in India

Design by Drew McCall

Contents

For David and Linsey,
in memory of Madeline Joy.

—Eric

Because everything that I have is yours, I humbly
dedicate this book to you, God. I put it back into the very
hands of the One who gave me the words to pen these
pages. I thank you that suffering is never for nothing,
and that this very book is proof of that. May it be not
only a guide for families walking through childhood
illness, hospitalizations, or child loss, but also a tool to
help them grow in their relationship with you.

—Jessika

Foreword

by Brad and Emily Jensen

We clutched each other's hands across the truck arm rest as we drove toward the big-city Emergency Room. Eye contact wasn't required to feel the blanket of tension, grief, and trepidation in the air.

Just ninety minutes earlier, we'd been trying to decide what to eat for dinner and when to leave for the pool when a phone conversation with our son's neurologist changed everything. He told us we needed to bring our son to the hospital, now. ("Oh and pack a bag, because he'll need to at least stay through the night.") So we dropped our pool towels and pulled a suitcase up from the basement. We called in backup and arranged for our other kids to stay the night with family. We loaded the suitcase into the truck, and we prepared—mentally, physically, and emotionally—for the battle ahead.

This wasn't our son's first seizure. By this point, we'd not only crossed the threshold of "strange medical event," we'd waded up to our knees in all things epilepsy. Daily medications and conversations about precautions, risks, seizure response training, and emergency plans were now as ordinary as talking about chicken nuggets and missing socks.

There wasn't much time to stop and analyze it—to think about what this was doing to our hearts, our faith, our marriage, our health, or our kids. When your child needs something and they are suffering, you just step in and do. You make the appointments and arrange the childcare and call the pharmacist. You stand up and step up and show up. But sooner or later, all that standing makes you tired and your knees start to tremble.

When your child has medical needs—long term or short term—where can you go to collapse? When the only place to sleep is a stuffy recliner next to the hospital bed, where can you go to rest?

You can go to the Lord.

After more than eight years of walking through diagnoses and disabilities with our son, and more than three years of adding epilepsy into the mix, we understand how that answer can be both frustrating and comforting. We've longed to not need rest because we've found a cure. We've wanted this journey to require fewer frantic night wakings and more vacations without kids, but it just... hasn't. Yes, we've had moments and even months of relief, but we've also had to carry a weight that is too heavy for us to bear. Yet in that, when no other answers or support have been able to hold us, we have found security in Christ and his promises.

And so, as we held hands in that truck on the way to the Emergency Room that evening, we had nothing else to do but open up our mouths and pray—knowing that God was listening, and he has always been faithful.

As you read about our story, perhaps there are elements you can relate to. Maybe the thought of Emergency Room visits and hospital recliners and ambulance sirens jolt your nervous system into action. Maybe you're deeply acquainted with the weight of words like "diagnosis" and "medication" and "doctor's appointment." It's likely that those come with difficult memories or future fears that make your shoulders tense, your jaw tighten, and your eyes fill with tears. But whether you're at the beginning of a journey you never wanted to be on in the first place, in the midst of a fog you're hoping to come out of, or decades along this weary road, we hope you're still open to hearing about how prayer matters in the midst of it.

The book you hold in your hands is a unique one. Because in all the other places that you've found words about suffering and fear and grief, we're pretty sure you haven't found specific prayers for the specific moments when you need words you don't have. Eric and Jessika have walked similar roads and have put words to some of the deepest longings and toughest moments a parent walking through a medical crisis can experience.

We're grateful for this book and will keep it nearby for the many moments when we're in need, and are too weak and unsure of how to articulate it. We hope that when you're all alone or clutching the hands of those you love, you'll open this book and remember you're in His.

Brad and Emily Jensen *live in central Iowa with their five children. They are small-business owners, and Emily is the author of multiple books, including* Risen Motherhood: Gospel Hope for Everyday Moments *and* He is Strong: Devotions for When You Feel Weak.

Introduction

Parents are always seeking to protect their children. We provide them with nutritious food, plan their schedules carefully, buy them the things they need and want—all so that they will flourish. From the very first scan in the womb, we hope and dream for them.

No parent hopes to walk through a medical crisis with their child. Extended illness, health complications, or loss are not in our plans for our little ones. So when we are thrust onto these unplanned journeys, we find them agonizing, bewildering, daunting, and debilitating.

We both know these realities well.

Jessika:
My son Ezra spent thirty-seven days in intensive care as a newborn and three additional days as a toddler. I remember feeling completely powerless as I sat idle at his bedside. I confess that though I desperately wanted to pray big, bold prayers as his life hung in the balance, I often felt too paralyzed to pray. Yet despite my shortcomings, I know nothing is wasted in God's hands.

Eric:
My wife and I have endured four miscarriages, each uniquely painful. In one instance, we discovered the pregnancy just before losing our baby. In another, we held our

child in our arms. We've faced the painful and frightening medical aspects of pregnancy loss.

Since then, both of us have walked alongside other bewildered, angry, and sorrowful parents, witnessing their faith and their doubts. Yet we've also seen God supply amazing strength, comfort, and healing to his suffering people.

If you are going through a medical crisis of any kind with your child or unborn baby, you are probably painfully aware of your limitations. All the work, worry, care, and attention you have given to your child seem to have made no difference. You suddenly feel that your life and your child's life are not in your hands. It is a terrifying feeling.

But even in the midst of these fears, there can be great comfort in knowing that we are in *his* hands—in God's hands.

Both of us know the suffering and fear that comes with serious threats to a child's health. But both of us also know the blessing of prayer, and the mercy of the God to whom we pray. We've written this book to help you know that blessing and that mercy, too.

IN TIME OF NEED

Consider these words from the Bible—verses which provide crucial answers to help us in a time of crisis.

For we do not have a high priest who is unable to sympathize with our weaknesses, but one who has been tempted in every way as we are, yet without sin.

Therefore, let us approach the throne of grace with boldness, so that we may receive mercy and find grace to help us in time of need. (Hebrews 4:15-16)

What is prayer?

Prayer means approaching the throne of grace—that is, God's throne. We come to him as weak children asking a parent for help. We ask boldly, because we trust in his love.

How can we know that God hears our prayers?

It's important to realize that nothing about us requires God to listen to us, much less answer us. We've all disobeyed, disregarded, and even despised God. Yet he has made a free choice to love us and invite us to be his children. He did this by sending his Son, Jesus—the "high priest" mentioned in Hebrews 4:15.

Jesus took on human nature, experiencing all the pain and weakness of a human life. Yet he lived the life we have all failed to live, flawlessly loving and obeying God the Father. Finally, he chose to die on our behalf—taking the punishment for the ways in which we all have disobeyed God. And God raised him from the dead as a sure sign that sin and death have been conquered.

We can pray because of Jesus. If we believe that Jesus lived, died, and rose in our place—if we trust in him— nothing can stop God loving us, or stand in the way of God hearing our prayers. It doesn't matter how weak we feel: if we trust in Jesus, we can know that God cares for us, listens to us, and is devoted to our eternal good. That is a wonderful thing to know when life is at its most confusing.

What can we pray for?

Hebrews 4:16 tells us that when we pray, we will "receive mercy and find grace to help us in time of need." Matthew 7:7-11 invites us to ask for any good thing. We can ask for healing, for strength, for peace, for help with practical needs. We can express our doubts and fears, ask for more faith, and pray for the people around us. Most of all, we can ask for God himself to be with us, and to work for our good and our child's good.

God will not always answer our prayers in the way we want him to. We won't necessarily be able to see why he is allowing things to take the course that they do. But there is something better: we can know that he loves us enough to die for us, and we can know that he is always answering our prayers in the way he knows is best for us and for his glory. That can give us great confidence to pray to God on our child's behalf.

WHEN YOU DON'T HAVE WORDS

Even so, sometimes prayer is hard. Sometimes, our souls are so exhausted that we can't put feelings into thoughts, much less thoughts into words. When that's the case, how can we pray?

The apostle Paul wrote an important but often overlooked truth: "We do not know what to pray for as we should" (Romans 8:26). If you find yourself there, don't be discouraged—even an apostle of Christ and a writer of Bible books knew that struggle! Yet Paul also knew this comfort: "Christ Jesus ... is at the right hand of God and intercedes for us" (v 34).

What a wonderful thought! Jesus is in heaven praying for us! No matter how weak and pathetic our prayers feel, we are well prayed for at God's throne.

There is other help too. God doesn't expect us to always use our own words when we pray to him (though he invites us to). He provided an entire book of prayers, the Psalms, that we can use as we speak to him. And he can use other believers—friends, family, pastors—to provide you with words to pray in the darkest times.

This book is our prayerful effort to supply you with words to pray when you don't have words. We've tried to offer prayers covering a variety of situations, concerns, and needs faced by those walking through childhood sickness and loss. Some of these won't apply to you; others will. Whichever prayers you choose, we are asking God to use them to help you come to his throne of grace with boldness—trusting in Jesus, and finding grace and mercy to help in this time of need.

Start by skimming the table of contents, asking the Spirit to lead you to the right prayers for you. We invite you to:

- *Pray personally.* Add the name of your child or specifics about your situation. (Phrases in *italics* invite you to personalize.) Add your own prayers in the margin or in your mind.
- *Pray with others.* Many of the prayers are written as "I" rather than "we," but you can also use them together. Each section also features a responsive reading

specifically designed for a group to pray together. You might use these as a family, or with a pastor or trusted friend.

• *Pray with your child.* Each section has a prayer specifically written for your child to pray, if they are of an age to do so. Many of the other prayers can also be said together. You may wish to pray some of them out loud as you sit with your child.

• *Pray in whatever way feels natural.* You may prefer to pray out loud or silently. You may pray through tears. We would advise praying slowly, reflecting on the words.

• *Pray with faith.* Know that Jesus loves you and gave himself for you. He is praying for you. He will work for your good.

OUR PRAYER FOR YOU

Good and gracious Father,

We pray that all who come to these pages
  find words that point them to the hope
  that is found in Jesus Christ the Lord
  and that help them to pray to you
  in the power of your Spirit.

Heal their children
  and their hearts.

Amen.

Jesus said,

"Leave the little children alone,

and don't try to keep them from coming to me,

because the kingdom of heaven

belongs to such as these."

Matthew 19:14

1

Prayers for Uncertain and Fearful Times

A Child's Prayer

Dear Jesus,

You invited children to come to you,
   so I am praying to ask you for help.

I am sick, and I am scared.

Something is wrong with my body,
   and I don't know what will happen.

Please, Jesus, heal me and give me peace.

Amen.

Matthew 19:13-15; John 5:1-9; John 6:16-21

For Peace

Jesus, wake up!

Out of nowhere,
  a storm has overtaken us.
We've been entirely caught off guard;
   we're totally ill-equipped.

The sky darkens.
The winds intensify.
The boat rocks violently.
The waves slam into our vessel.

Jesus, wake up!

The storm is raging now.
The wind and the rain are like
   bullets pelting us relentlessly.
We are scared we won't make it.

Prince of Peace, rebuke the storm.
Rebuke the wind, the rain, and the waves.
Command them to be still in your holy authority.
Speak peace over our circumstances.
Speak peace over our minds.

Jesus, we call on you
   because you can.

––––––––––––––

Matthew 8:23-27

For Wisdom and Clarity

We do not know what to do, but we look to you.

Lord, this situation is beyond us;
    we don't understand what's happening.
We face a thousand questions
    and don't know where to find answers.
The counsel of professionals is over our heads,
    and the advice of family and friends confuses us.

We do not know what to do, but we look to you.

You are the only wise God!
    Yes, the depth of your wisdom is unsearchable!
You founded the earth by wisdom
    and established the heavens by understanding.
No one directed you or gave you counsel;
    no one taught you how to be wise.

We do not know what to do, but we look to you;
    we ask for wisdom in faith, without doubting,
    because we know that you give to all
    generously and ungrudgingly.

We do not know what to do, but we look to you.

---

2 Chronicles 20:12; Romans 16:27; 11:33-34;
Proverbs 3:19-20; Isaiah 40:12-14; James 1:5

For a Clear Diagnosis

God of creation,
　　you make no mistakes.
You are altogether perfect.
　　All your works are wonderful.

But, Lord, we live in a world that is
　　corrupted by disease, decay, and death.
Our child is not well, and we don't know why.
　　The medical team is seeking to find the cause.
Lord, in your mercy, give us a correct diagnosis.

God, you knit this child together carefully,
　　and you know exactly what's wrong,
　　so we pray for an accurate diagnosis.
Even if it is not what we want to hear,
　　give us strength to walk the road
　　that you have prepared for us.

Holy Spirit, guard our hearts from despair.
Transform our thoughts so that
　　we might hope and trust in you
　　no matter what the diagnosis may be
　　or the future may hold.
Equip and empower us to
　　run the race you have set for us
　　with wholehearted devotion and faith.

_____

Psalm 139

For Trusting God and Relinquishing Control

Father,

I love *my child*! Oh, how I love *my child*!
   I want to do all I can for *my child*.
But what I can do and what you can do
   are two very different things.
You are God; I am not.

I confess that I am distracted by many tasks,
   worried and upset about many things.
Far too often, my busyness betrays my belief
   that I am in control.

My mind is always there with *my child*,
   whether I'm at home or at the hospital.
I spend time thinking about what might be wrong.
   I administer care, day in, day out.

I sometimes think and act as though
   if I have all the information,
   if I make the best choices,
   if I do all the right things,
   if I am always present,
   then maybe I can guarantee the result I desire.
I do all this out of faith in myself.

Lord, I confess that I am an idol to myself.
   I fall into believing that I can interpret the past

and make sense of the present
so as to control the future.

My desire for control is the height of foolishness,
revealing the depths of my lack of trust in you.
A thousand nights of worrying
have never added one moment to my life span.

Father, forgive my pride and fill me with faith in you.

Ravens don't sow or reap; yet you feed them.
Flowers don't labor or sew; yet you clothe them.
You love *my child* more
than the birds and the flowers—
so keep me from living as though you don't.
It makes you happy, Father,
to give us your kingdom—
so help me not to be anxious and afraid
but to trust and treasure you.

Father, if you gave up your Son to make me yours,
then I can trust you with *my child*.
I cannot relinquish control, for I never had control.
But I can trust you—and I do.

Luke 10:38-42; 12:22-31; Romans 8:32

Do not fear,

for I am with you;

do not be afraid,

for I am your God.

Isaiah 41:10

When Our Faith Feels Shaky

Lord, you are the Good Shepherd, and we are your sheep.
This dark valley has left us frail and vulnerable.
Hear our cries!

Our adversary is prowling like a lion,
   ready to pounce and devour.
He tempts us in this wilderness,
   offering us false promises and twisting your word.

Strengthen us with your vast power
   and clothe us with your armor
   so that we can resist the devil
   by being firm in our faith.

Like a belt, the truth of Jesus surrounds us.
Like a breastplate, Christ's righteousness covers us.
Like sandals, the gospel of peace equips us for this road.
Like a shield, faith stops the lies of the evil one.
Like a helmet, your salvation guards us.
Like a sword, your word fights for us.

By faith, we claim the victory of Jesus.
By faith, we renounce Satan and all his demonic forces.
By faith, we stand alert, constantly praying in hope
   because Jesus crushed Satan's head
   and will soon crush him under our feet.

---

1 Peter 5:8-9; Matthew 4:1-11; Ephesians 6:10-20; Romans 16:20

When My Thoughts Overwhelm Me

Jesus,

It feels like everyone and everything
   is trying to tell me what to think.

Doctors, nurses, and statistics;
family, friends, and neighbors;
the devil and my sinful flesh;
the world and the church—
each of these press thoughts on me,
   some honorable, some deplorable,
   some hopeful, some doubtful,
   some helpful, some hurtful,
   some pure, some sinful,
   some true, some false.

Lord, to whom shall I go?
You have the words of eternal life.

By your Spirit, equip me to think rightly,
   to take captive and demolish
   every thought that opposes
   the true knowledge of you.

Do not let my thoughts be conformed to the world,
   but transform me by renewing my mind,
   so that I may clearly discern what is
   your good, pleasing, and perfect will.

Renew the spirit of my mind by your Holy Spirit,
teaching me to throw off corruption and deceit,
giving me a new mind that dwells on you.
Set my mind on things above,
not on earthly things.

Yes, Jesus, teach me to think about you
because you are the embodiment of what is
honorable, just, pure, lovely, and commendable.

Teach me to present all my thoughts to you in prayer
so that your peace, which surpasses understanding,
may guard my heart and mind in you.
And may the thoughts of my heart
be acceptable to you, Lord Jesus,
my rock and my Redeemer.

John 6:68; 2 Corinthians 10:3-6; Romans 12:2; Ephesians 4:20-24;
Colossians 3:2; Philippians 4:4-9; Psalm 19:14

When I Am Fearful

Go away, fear. You have no power here.

I trust in God the Father, who loves me
  and sent his Son to save me.

I trust in God the Son, who loves me
  and gave his life for me.

I trust in God the Spirit, who loves me
  and is making me new.

Go away, fear. You have no power here.

———————————

Psalm 56; Psalm 27

For a Clear Sense of the Lord's Presence

As a child longs for its mother's face,
    Father, we want to see you.
Open our eyes to the supernatural.
Comfort our anxious thoughts and ease worried minds
    as you give us vision to see you at work on our behalf.

As a child longs for its mother's touch,
    Father, we want to feel you.
Envelop us in your peace
    as we feel your righteous right hand steadying us
    and your holy presence surrounding us.

As a child longs for its mother's voice,
    Father, we want to hear you.
Tune our ears to new frequencies.
Give us divine counsel
    as you speak wisdom into our circumstances.

---

2 Kings 6:15-17; Isaiah 41:10; 1 Kings 19:11-13

Don't worry about anything, but in everything,
through prayer and petition with thanksgiving,
present your requests to God. And the peace of
God, which surpasses all understanding, will
guard your hearts and minds in Christ Jesus.

Philippians 4:6-7

A Responsive Prayer: We Believe

There is a responsive prayer like this in every section. The parts printed in bold type are designed to be said by the whole group. The parts printed in regular type are designed to be said by the leader only.

Leader

The Lord God said,
  I declare the end from the beginning,
  and from long ago what is not yet done,
  saying: my plan will take place,
  and I will do all my will.

All

Lord, the future is not uncertain with you;
  you are not afraid of what will happen next.
But the future is uncertain to us, Lord;
  we are fearful of what will happen next.

The Lord Jesus said,
  I am going away and I am coming to you.
  I have told you now before it happens
  so that when it does happen you may believe.

We believe, Lord, that Jesus went away
  through the cross, death, and the grave,
  offering himself as the atonement for our sin.
We believe, Lord, that Jesus returned
  through the resurrection from the dead,
  conquering sin, death, and the devil.

We believe, Lord, that Jesus will come back
    to raise us from the dead in glory
    to reign with him in a new world.

The Lord Jesus said,
    Peace I leave with you. My peace I give to you.
    Don't let your heart be troubled or fearful.

We believe, Lord, that these things are certain:
    Christ has died.
    Christ has risen.
    Christ will come again.
We believe that these things guarantee our peace
    even when we don't know
    what tomorrow will bring.

The Lord Jesus said,
    Don't let your heart be troubled.
    Believe in God; believe also in me.

We believe; help our unbelief!

Isaiah 46:10; John 14:1, 27; Mark 9:24

2

Prayers for Healing

A Child's Prayer

Dear Jesus,

Everyone says you're a healer.
They say nothing is impossible for you.

They tell me Bible stories of how you healed
   with a word
   or with a touch.

I believe the Jesus of the Bible
   is the same Jesus that is with me now.

Jesus, please, will you shout "Leave!"
   and command the sickness to go?
Would you place your hand on my body
   and make everything right again?

I believe you can heal me, Jesus.
I do.

Amen.

_____

Luke 7:1-10; 5:12-13

For a Miracle

Jesus,

No matter where you went, crowds gathered.
    The sick.
    The lame.
    The blind.
    The deaf.
    The broken.
    The plagued.
    The tortured.
    The desperate.

They followed you in hope, for healing was in your wings.
It flowed from your mouth, your clothes,
    and your hands.

So just as the woman crawled through a crowd to touch
    the tassel that hung at your feet,
    just as the centurion sent others to petition you,
so, with humility and bold faith,
    we come praying for our own miracle.

Jesus, touch *our child* and heal *our child* supernaturally.
Speak a word of healing over *our child* and let it be so.
May this prayer of faith rise to the heavens
    and touch your ear.
May *our child* be healed in your holy name.

Matthew 15:30; Luke 5:12-26; Luke 8:40-56; Luke 7:1-10; Malachi 4:2

For an Unborn Child

The womb is a secret and hidden place—
   but not to you, Father.

When John the Baptist
   was in his mother's womb,
   you caused him to leap for joy
   at the presence of the Lord in Mary's womb.

You are also at work in this womb,
   knitting our child together in wondrous ways.

We fear for the life of our unborn child.

Please guard, sustain, heal and safely deliver
   this little one, who is made in your image,
   and keep us trusting in your wise and good decree.

_____

Psalm 139:13-16; Luke 1:39-45

For an Infant or Toddler

Lord, you have never taken your eyes off *my child*.

Even in the womb, you held *my child* in your hands;
   his/her unformed body was never hidden from you.

You sustained *my child* from the womb into the world
   and carried *him/her* along since birth.

You made no mistakes when you formed *my child*.
You knew *my child* would experience this
   before *he/she* was conceived—
   for you know all our days in advance.
So, this was no surprise to you after birth.

Please have mercy on *my child*—
   relieve suffering and grant comfort,
   restore health and give full healing.

_____

Psalm 139:13-16; Isaiah 53:5

For an Older Child

Jesus,

You love children.
To you, they are not an inconvenience.
They matter greatly.
You make time for them.
You welcome them into your loving arms
    and you bless them.

Lord, we bring our precious child
    before your throne of grace.
We humbly petition for the blessing of healing on earth,
    just as it will be in heaven.

———————

Matthew 19:14

They put them at his feet,

and he healed them.

Matthew 15:30

For Our Unbelief

Jesus, when a man asked you to heal his daughter,
   you said, "Don't be afraid. Only believe."

I'm asking you to heal my child,
   but I am afraid and filled with unbelief.

Help me.
Show me compassion.
For you know I am made of dust.

I do believe; help my unbelief!

Mark 5:36-43; Psalm 103:13-18; Mark 9:14-29

When There Seems to Be No Hope
(Based on Psalm 73)

Oh, Lord!

The prognosis is not good.
No healing is in sight.
Death approaches.
I am hopeless.

You are indeed good to your people.
But as for me, my feet are slipping,
   my steps are going astray.

I envy the wicked and arrogant
   who are not suffering like me.
Have I turned from my sin
   and trusted in you
   for nothing?

When I try to make sense of this,
   it seems hopeless.

When my heart is wounded
   and without understanding,
I become embittered,
   like a foolish animal.

But when I look to your sanctuary in heaven—
   at the crucified and resurrected Jesus—
I gain understanding.

In Christ, I am not without hope:
    in Christ, I have you, my heavenly Father.

You are always with me.
You hold my hand.
You guide me in your wisdom.
You guarantee resurrection glory.

Lord, let this hope inspire endurance
    so that when my flesh and heart fail,
you are the strength of my heart,
    my portion forever.

As for me, your presence is my good.
I have made you my refuge, Lord,
    so I can proclaim all you do.

Ephesians 2:12-13; 1 Thessalonians 1:3; 4:13-18

A Responsive Prayer: The Lord Assures Us
(Based on Psalm 103:1-5; Isaiah 53:4-5; James 5:13-15)

Leader
My soul, bless the Lord,
   and all that is within me, bless his holy name.

All
My soul, bless the Lord,
   and do not forget all his benefits.

He forgives all your iniquity;
   he heals all your diseases.
He redeems your life from the Pit;
   he crowns you with faithful love and compassion.
He satisfies you with good things;
   your youth is renewed like the eagle.

The Lord died so that we might be healed.

He himself bore our sicknesses,
   and he carried our pains;
but we in turn regarded him stricken,
   struck down by God, and afflicted.

But he was pierced because of our rebellion,
   crushed because of our iniquities;
punishment for our peace was on him,
   and we are healed by his wounds.

The Lord instructs us to pray for the sick:

Is anyone among you suffering?
He should pray.

Is anyone among you sick?
He should call for the elders of the church,
and they are to pray over him,
anointing him with oil in the name of the Lord.

The Lord assures us:
The prayer of faith will save the sick person,
and the Lord will raise him up.

Is it really right to have such confidence?
Not everyone will be healed in this life.
Yet this *is* the confidence we have before him:
If we ask anything according to his will, he hears us.

So, we pray:

Dear Lord, we approach you in faith
on behalf of *our child,*
asking you to heal *her/him* of *this affliction,*
not for our sake but to display your glory.
Not our will but yours be done.

We know that you have heard us, Lord Jesus,
and we trust that you will do
what is right and good.

Amen.

Job 1:21; Luke 7:6-9; 11:9-10; 1 John 5:14-15

3

Prayers for Our Child

A Child's Prayer

Dear God,

The doctors say something is wrong
  and my body isn't working right.
They are trying to fix me and take away my pain.

But God, I'm scared.
  I am scared of what might happen.

God, I'm confused, too.
I don't understand why this is happening
  to my family and to me.

The Bible says your perfect love pushes out fear.
God, let your perfect love fill my soul
  and destroy my fears.

The Bible also says we should
  give our worries to you because you care.
God, you can have them all—
  take my worries and give me peace.

God, be with me. Help me.

Amen.

---

1 John 4:18; 1 Peter 5:7

For Comfort and Relief from Pain

Father of mercies,

I know that you not only see *my child*,
    you are near in *his/her* suffering.

Just as your Spirit hovered over the darkness
    of an unformed earth,
    you are hovering over *my child* right now.

Just as the cross made a way to save generations
    from eternal death,
I pray that you would work to bring *my child* relief
    from *his/her* present sufferings.

May your plans for *my child* be for good
    and not for harm.

Psalm 34:17-18; Genesis 1:2; Jeremiah 29:11

For Courage

Father,

Today's sufferings
and tomorrow's uncertainty
threaten to conquer *my child*.

Help *her/him* to be courageous
knowing that Jesus has
conquered the world.

Amen.

———

John 16:33

May the LORD bless you and protect you;
may the LORD make his face shine on you
and be gracious to you;
may the LORD look with favor on you
and give you peace.

Numbers 6:24-26

For Joy

Lord, this trial is more than *my child* can bear.

Though *my child's* weeping lasts
  for more than a night,
  and tears fill *his/her* eyes and blur *his/her* vision,
help *my child* to fix *his/her* eyes
  on the promises found in your word.

Your everlasting joy is strength.
Your mercies are new each morning
  and with them come unexplainable joy.

Position *my child's* heart to see all the good you are doing
  in *his/her* life.

Fill *my child* with your unspeakable joy
  so that *he/she* may lift *his/her* hands in praise to you,
  even in suffering.

———

Psalm 30:5

For Understanding

As heaven is higher than the earth,
   so your ways are higher than our ways,
   and your thoughts than our thoughts, O Lord.
So, how could a child understand
   what is happening to them?

Help *my child* understand this situation
   to whatever extent *she/he* is able.
But above all, help *my child*
   to understand that you, Lord,
   are always wise
   and good.

———————

Isaiah 55:8-9

For Peace

Father, turn *my child's* eyes from
  his/her current circumstances,
  and fix *his/her* thoughts on you.

Help *him/her* to trust you, Lord,
  even when it doesn't make sense.

Keep *my child's* mind, body, and spirit
  in your perfect peace.

———————

Isaiah 26:3

For Perseverance
(Based on Psalm 13)

How long, Lord?
Will you forget *my child* forever?
How long must *she/he* endure
   weakness,
   physical agony,
   painful treatments,
   relentless appointments,
   and separation from loved ones?
How long will sickness dominate *her/him*?

Consider *my child* and answer, Lord my God.
Restore brightness to *her/his* eyes.

Lord, teach *my child* to trust in your faithful love;
   let *her/his* heart rejoice in your deliverance
   and sing to you because you treated *her/him* generously.

For Protection

Lord God,
    just as you dwelt with your people in the wilderness
    as a pillar of cloud by day and a pillar of fire by night
    to guard and protect them at all times,
be with my child.

Strengthen *my child* and guard *him/her* from the evil one.
Surround *him/her*.
Hem *him/her* in.

Rescue *my child*, for *he/she* loves you.
Protect *my child*, for *he/she* trusts in your name.
Answer *my child*, for *he/she* calls on you.
Be with *my child*, for *he/she* is in trouble.

Save my child.
Honor my child.
Reward my child with long life and salvation.

---

2 Thessalonians 3:3; Psalm 139:5 (ESV); Psalm 91

For Rest

Lord, you are the Good Shepherd.
Even though *my child* walks through this dark valley,
we are not afraid, because you go with *her/him*.
You lead *my child* to lush green pastures,
    and stand watch as you command *her/him* to rest.
As *my child* closes *her/his* eyes and drifts off,
    you renew *her/his* strength.

———

Psalm 23

I will say to the LORD, "My refuge and my

fortress, my God, in whom I trust."

Psalm 91:2 (ESV)

For Trust in Jesus

Lord God,

In the goodness of the creation,
   you called humans
   to trust in you.

In the wake of sin and death,
   you called sinners
   to trust in you.

In your covenant with Abraham,
   you called him
   to trust in you.

In the wilderness and the promised land
   you called Israel
   to trust in you.

In the promise of an eternal king,
   you called David
   to trust in you.

In their long and painful exile
   you called your people
   to trust in you.

In the fulfillment of all your promises
   you call everyone
   to trust in Jesus.

In answering my prayers, O Lord,
please cause *my child*
to trust in Jesus.

In your grace, help *him/her* to trust in Jesus Christ—
to receive salvation
through Jesus' death for *my child's* sins
and Jesus' resurrection from the dead.

In hope, help *my child* to trust that you are
working everything together for *his/her* good.

In every circumstance, help *him/her* to trust that
neither death nor life,
nor sickness nor suffering,
nor things now or things in the future
will be able to separate *him/her*
from your love in Christ Jesus our Lord.

Romans 8:28-39

For Defying the Odds

Lord, you are the Great Physician.

Certainly you use doctors to work wonders for your glory.
But like us, they see through a clouded lens.
They don't have full access to your infinite wisdom.
You, and you alone, are God.
You have the final say.

You know *my child* intimately
   because you created *her/him*.
You know *my child's* purpose
   because you have given it.
You know the plans you have for *my child*
   because you have designed them.

Regardless of the diagnosis delivered, we will look to you,
   for you have the final word.

Whatever prognosis is given,
   I will wait for your direction,
   for you number all our days.

If it is your will, let *my child* defy the odds.
And to you will be the glory forever and ever, amen.

Jeremiah 29:11; Psalm 139

A Responsive Prayer: You Know

Leader
Our Father in heaven,
You know what it is like to be a parent.

All
You have a Son you love deeply.
You witnessed his sufferings.
You watched him die.
You know.

You are our Father.
You made us in the womb.
You called us to be born again.
You adopted us as sons and daughters in Christ.
You made us your children through your Son's death.

We come in faith, believing that you, Father,
    will not give stones when we ask for bread;
    will not give a snake when we ask for a fish.
For you are a good and righteous Father
    who gives good things to those who ask him.

Your Son invited little children to come to him.
We invite you to come to our little child
    to see *his/her* suffering
    and be compassionate.

End sadness; grant joy.
End pain; bring comfort.
End tossings; give sleep.
End fear; stir up courage.
End anxiety; create peace.
End sickness; bring healing.
End uncertainty; give assurance.
End confusion; give understanding.
End doubting; produce hope in Jesus.

We ask this, Father, in the name of your Son.

Amen.

Matthew 7:7-12

4

Prayers for Our Family

If you then, who are evil, know how to give
good gifts to your children, how much more
will your Father in heaven give good
things to those who ask him.

Matthew 7:11

A Child's Prayer

God, you are the giver of good gifts.
Thank you for the gift of my family.
Thank you for creating each person and each personality.
Thank you that of all the people in the world,
    you chose these people to be my family.

Lord, I am sick, and everyone is praying for me.
Help me to pray for them too.
Help us to grow closer during this difficult time
    and let us love one another like you love us.

Amen.

———

James 1:17

For Help in Parenting Other Children
(Based on Psalm 127)

Father, I know children are a heritage from you—
    the fruit of the womb is a reward.
I thank you for *my children*,
    and the gift they are.

I don't underestimate the enormous responsibility
    of parenting *my children*.
I realize that, like arrows in the hand of a warrior,
    children must be carefully shaped,
    stewarded and well cared for,
    placed and guided upon the right paths,
    and eventually released to fly on their own.

O, Lord, I want to honor you as I parent *my children* well.
I want to honor and glorify you.

In this time of suffering,
    when my every thought and action
    seem to center around *my sick child*,
I ask for you to open my eyes to *my other children*.
Help me to really see them.
Give me divine access into their hearts.
Reveal their struggles.
Pour out your infinite wisdom.
Guide my steps as I navigate this season of parenthood.

For Growth in Our Faith

Our family has grown through this suffering, Lord.

We've grown in our fear
   of suffering, sickness, sorrow, and death.

We've grown in our knowledge
   of tests, diagnoses, causes, and cures.

But, Lord, more than anything else, we want to grow
   in our faith in you
   and our knowledge of you.

Remind us again of who you are:
   the God who made us and sustains us,
   the God who seeks us and calls us to yourself,
   the God who redeems us and raises us to new life,
   the God who says,
   "I will never leave you or abandon you."

Faith comes from hearing the message about Christ,
   who died for our sins
   and rose from the dead to save us.
So cause the word of Christ to dwell richly among us,
   so that our roots might go deep into the gospel
   to build us up in him and establish our faith.

Hebrews 13:5; Romans 10:17; Colossians 2:7; 3:16

For Grace for One Another

Lord, you are the God who makes me holy—
   Jehovah M'Kaddesh.

When I am tempted to blame,
   to lash out,
   to complain,
   to write off,
may the mercy and grace you extend to me
   overflow and be poured out onto others.

When my grace runs out,
   may you be my ever-sufficient source.

---

2 Corinthians 12:9; Leviticus 20:8; 2 Thessalonians 2:13

But he said to me,

"My grace is sufficient for you,

for my power is perfected in weakness."

Therefore, I will most gladly boast all

the more about my weaknesses, so that

Christ's power may reside in me.

2 Corinthians 12:9

For the Mother

Lord God, when Simeon said,
   "A sword will pierce your own soul,"
   did Mary understand the weight
   of that prophesied suffering?
Could she have had any idea of the magnitude
   of the sorrow and pain
   she would experience
   through the life and death of her precious son, Jesus?

Lord, how did she do it?
How did she shift her eyes from her son's
   immense suffering
   and fix them on you and your divine plans?

Abba, Father,
Nothing can prepare a mother's heart
   for the indescribable, searing pain
   of seeing her child in such a state.
This mother is watching her child suffer things
   she never imagined.
Her soul feels crushed, her spirit downcast
   and unable to go on.

God of mercy,
   lavish your love upon *this mother*
   who helplessly looks on as *her child* suffers.
Bestow upon her your supernatural peace
   which surpasses all understanding.

Lead her to you, the rock that is higher than herself.
Be her strong tower against the enemy.
Provide her refuge under your wings.
Strengthen her with the truth of your word.
Let praise fall from her lips, always.

_____

Luke 2:35; Psalm 61

For the Father

Father,

You know what it means for a father
    to watch his child suffer,
    for you saw your own Son, Jesus, on the cross.

So help *this father* as he watches his child suffer now,
    and deliver him from every temptation
    to cope in unhealthy ways.

Deliver *this father* from all unrighteousness
    and make him a father who is like you.

You are the Father of mercies and the God of all comfort.
Help him be a merciful comforter to his family.

You value your children more than birds and flowers.
    Cause him to love his children more
    than the things of earth.

You give good gifts to your children.
    Fill his heart with happy generosity
    toward his children.

You reveal the truth about Jesus to your children.
    Help him tell his children about your Son.

Matthew 6:25-34; 7:7-11; 2 Corinthians 1:3-4

For My Other Children

Jesus, I know your heart for children.
You welcome them without inhibition.

I picture you,
    humbly squatting down to their level,
    arms open and inviting,
    with warm, understanding eyes of compassion.

I pray that your open arms attract *my children*
    like a magnet.
As they are pulled into your embrace,
    do what only you can do, Lord.
Fill in any gaps in their care that I may have missed
    as I focus our attention on *my child*.
Pour out your love and compassion onto them.

You know everything;
receive their every concern,
    even the ones unspoken and unknown to me.
You can do anything;
    calm their every worry with your supernatural peace.
In your endless mercy, catch their every tear
    and provide comfort for their souls.
Be their refuge and their safe place
    as you invite them to sit in your lap
    and remain in your embrace.

Matthew 19:14

For Grandparents

Father,

Thank you for *my child's* grandparents,
  and for the love they have for *her/him*.

In this season I pray
  you'll not only comfort *my child's grandparents*
  but that you'll draw them near to you in faith
  and use them in mighty ways.

Equip them to serve,
  enable them to uplift,
  use them for your glory.

––––––––––

Proverbs 16:31

For Compassion toward One Another

Jesus,

When you saw the crowds, you felt compassion for them,
    because they were distressed and dejected.
See our family's pain and show us mercy.

Teach us, Savior, to see each other's sufferings
    and to have compassion for one another.

Guard our relationships against neglect and selfishness;
    teach us to see where other family members are weak
    so that we may bear their burdens.

Help us, as parents, to remember that
    our children are children:
    young, tender, and weak,
    in need of our kindness and help.

Keep our children from becoming hard-hearted
    in this journey,
    growing bitter toward distracted parents or a sick sibling.
Fill them, instead, with grace for each other.

Bless our family with your compassion,
    so that we might bless each other
    with the same compassion.

———————

Matthew 9:35-38

For Help to Encourage One Another in Faith

Lord,
  when the families of Israel journeyed in the wilderness,
  though you fed them each day with manna,
they grumbled against you and against Moses—
  failing to love their God and their neighbor.
Growing impatient, they did not persevere
  because they did not have faith.

In my journey, don't let me be like faithless Israel,
  grumbling against you and against others,
  refusing to wait on you in my unbelief
  and discouraging others from believing.

Instead, make me like one of your faithful prophets
  who spoke your promises to your people,
  and who were examples of suffering and patience;
  they persevered and were blessed by you,
  their compassionate and merciful Lord.

Fix my eyes on Jesus, who, for the joy set before him,
  endured such great suffering and yet finished the race.

As I look to Jesus, encourage my heart
  so that I will point others to Jesus
  for help and comfort on the way.

James 5:10-11; Hebrews 12:1-3

A Responsive Prayer:
You Are Our Father

Leader

We are a family under pressure, facing fear and suffering,
   and yet we have hope in our heavenly Father!
See what great love the Father has given us
   that we should be called God's children—and we are!

All

**We are God's children now because God sent his Son
   to redeem us from our sin and give us adoption.**

And because we are his children,
   God sent the Spirit of his Son
   into our hearts, crying, "Abba! Father!"

**Since we are God's children through Christ
   we have the freedom of children
   to ask our Father for what we need.**

Our Father in Heaven,
   your plan of salvation is one of family-making.

**You are our Father; we are your children.
Christ is the bridegroom; the church is his bride.
Jesus is our brother; we are siblings in your household.**

We want our family to look like your family—
   to show the world how good it is
   to be in the household of God.

Forgive us, Father, for how we've failed:
  We're unloving and neglectful,
  self-centered and resentful,
  short-tempered and angry,
  unthoughtful and unkind.

So, we kneel before you, the Father
  who names every family in heaven and on earth,
  praying that, according to the riches of your glory,
  you would strengthen each of us
  in our inner being through your Spirit,
  that Christ may dwell in our hearts through faith.

May our family be rooted
  and firmly established in love,
  able to comprehend the greatness of your love,
  and to know the all-surpassing love of Christ,
  so that we may be filled with all the fullness of you.

Now to him who is able to do above and beyond
  all that we ask or think
  according to the power that works in us—
  to him be glory in our family and in Christ Jesus
  to all generations, forever and ever. Amen.

Galatians 4:4-7; Ephesians 3:14-21; 1 John 3:1

5

Prayers for the Medical Team

A Child's Prayer

God,
   you are Lord of all.
You know everything
   because you created everything.

I know being in your hands is the best place to be.
   You hold me in safety.
   And you hold my medical team too.

Help my medical team—
   give them everything they need
   to care for me.

I trust your perfect plan.

Amen.

———

Isaiah 41:10

For the Care Team

Father God,

Please guide the selection of *my child's* care team.

Appoint and anoint
   those who are humble in heart,
   those who are skilled and competent,
   those who choose to listen to your voice,
   those who are committed to doing your will.

Bless *my child's* care team as they care for *him/her*.
Bless them as they submit to you and your will.

———

1 John 2:20

For the Doctors

O God, you are the Lord, my Shepherd—Jehovah Rohi.
As you skillfully and compassionately care for the flock,
   teach *my child's* doctors how to care for *her/him*.

Guide *my child's* doctors.
Provide them with supernatural wisdom.
Give them fresh revelation
   into *my child's* circumstances.
Lead *my child's* doctors onto paths of righteousness
   for your name's sake and for your glory.

———

Psalm 23

For the Nurses

Jesus,
    thank you for the nurses you have placed in our path
    and the ones you have entrusted to care for *my child*.
I see the calling you have placed on their lives.

I pray a blessing over these nurses today
    and in the days to come.
May they be blessed exceedingly and abundantly more
    than they can imagine
for their obedience and diligence in caring for *my child*.

Bless the nurses whose hearts are humble,
    who serve day-in and day-out
    doing the hard, the messy, and the holy,
    and who expect nothing in return.

Bless the nurses whose words and actions are gentle,
    who tenderly care for *my child*
    as if *he/she* were their own,
    and who speak life and encouragement into our hearts.

Bless the nurses who extend mercy,
    who meet us where we are in our shock and grief
    and who don't take offense
    at the things we might say or do.

Bless them to receive endless mercy.

Matthew 5:1-10

For the Transport Team

God Almighty—El Shaddai—
　command your angels to guard *my child*
　and *my child's* transport team.

Protect and defend them in all your ways.
Lift them up and into your hands,
　carrying them safely to their destination.

———————

Psalm 91:11-12

For the Surgeon

O Lord,

You fashioned the first man from the dust.
You fashioned me in my mother's womb.
You know the body of *my child* perfectly—
   you know what is broken
   and how to repair it.

Lord, I ask you to bless the hands and the mind
   of the surgeon you have chosen to serve *my child*.
Give this surgeon wisdom, insight, and skill,
   and work through *her/his* hands
   to heal my child.

———————

Genesis 2:7

Happy is the one

whose help is the God of Jacob,

whose hope is in the Lord his God,

the Maker of heaven and earth,

the sea and everything in them.

He remains faithful forever.

Psalm 146:5-6

For Unity in Decision-Making

Father,

I thank you for the medical team
   that you have given
   to care for *my child*.

Give them unity as they make decisions,
   for plans fail when there is no counsel,
   but they succeed with many advisers.

Grant each person abundant humility to
   value the contributions of others,
   set aside concern for self-glory,
   know their own limitations,
   admit their mistakes,
   listen and learn.

Remind them that they are on the same team,
   working toward the same objective—
   the healing of *my child.*

Amen.

Proverbs 15:22

For Divine Wisdom

Lord,

You alone are wise
    and never in need of counsel.

You give wisdom;
    from your mouth
    come knowledge and understanding.

So I come before you in faith,
    calling out for insight and understanding,
    asking for wisdom for *my child's* medical team.

Give them great wisdom—
    generously and ungrudgingly—
    to discern between truth and error,
    to choose what is good and helpful.

To you—the only wise God—
    be glory forever!

Amen.

Proverbs 2:3-6; James 1:5-8; Romans 16:27

For Undistracted Minds

Father, I know how many distractions
　　I face while caring for *my child*.

I cannot imagine how many distractions
　　this medical team faces each day
　　as they care for multiple children
　　in addition to their own lives.

Remove distractions
　　and enable them to focus
　　on each assignment in turn.

Help them not to worry about the next task,
for each task has enough trouble of its own.

Remind them that worry is powerless,
　　unable to change a single thing.

May they trust you in each moment
　　and learn to turn to you for help.

Amen.

Matthew 6:25-34

For the Hospital Community

Jesus, I praise you for your compassion for the sick!
You welcomed all those who were sick with diseases.
You laid your hands on each one, and you healed them.

Your merciful heart is on display in this hospital,
    where those who are sick with various diseases
    are welcomed, loved, comforted, and cared for—
    a gift of grace from you.

Bless this hospital, Lord, to serve the sick well,
    through leaders of integrity, skilled administrators,
    diligent staff, and competent medical professionals.

Guard this hospital against all evil.
Expose corruption, correct incompetence,
    establish justice.

Make this place a means of your grace
so that each patient turns to you in thanksgiving and trust.

Help me, Lord Jesus, to be a witness for you here.
Lead me to displays of kindness
    that demonstrate your love.
And give me opportunities with many people in this place
    to speak about who you are
    and what you have done for me
    through your death and resurrection.

Luke 4:40

A Responsive Prayer:
For Their Hands

Leader

The Lord, in his goodness and mercy,
   has not left us to suffer without help,
   but has given us the gift of medical care,
   which comes to us through the ministry of people—
   doctors, nurses, surgeons, specialists,
   and many more.

Therefore, we thank God for them and pray for them.

All

Thank you, Lord, for giving us this medical team;
   for giving them the necessary
   skill, wisdom, and training
   to fulfill their calling.

We pray for their hands.
Keep their hands from doing harm.
Use their hands to heal and nurture.

We pray for their minds.
Give them clarity of thought that they may
   utilize research,
   diagnose correctly,
   calculate with accuracy,
   give clear and right orders.

Help them discern the pain and needs
 of children who cannot communicate
 their needs as clearly as adults do.
Make them sensitive to the needs of the family.

We pray for their ears.
May they listen to each other in humility
 seeking to learn and understand
 for the benefit of the patient.

We pray for their mouths.
Help them speak words of comfort
 and to deliver updates
 with accuracy and compassion.
Guard their lips against wrong, hurtful,
 or insensitive remarks.

We pray for their hearts.
Fill them with humility, patience, and compassion.
Help them to be merciful to all.

The Lord is good to everyone;
 his compassion rests on all he has made.

All you have made will thank you, Lord;
 the faithful will bless you.

———————

Psalm 145:9-10

6

Prayers for the Things We Need

A Child's Prayer

Lord, you are the God who provides what we need—
  nothing is impossible for you.

Even if I don't speak the words aloud,
  you know what every member of my family needs.

Lord, I pray that you won't just meet our needs,
  but that you'll do more than we ask,
  because that's the kind of God you are.

Amen.

Ephesians 3:20

For Wisdom to Prioritize

Lord, my responsibilities overwhelm me.
I have no idea where to start.

Help me trust in you with my heart
and not rely on my own understanding.

Make me know you in all my ways,
for you will make my paths straight.

Give me the wisdom to know
what to do today,
what to do tomorrow,
what to give to others,
and what to leave undone.

———————

Proverbs 3:5-6

For the Ability to Attend
to Responsibilities

Father,
    though time seems to stand still here in this room,
    the world outside these walls has never missed a beat.

My fast-paced life hasn't paused;
    instead, it has raged on.
I wonder, how will I ever catch up?

My responsibilities haven't waited for me;
    rather, they have piled up.
I question, how will I get everything done?

Lord, set my mind on things above,
    not on the things of this earth.
Set my mind on your sufficiency.

Remind me that it is in my weakness
    that your power is made perfect.
Through your supernatural grace,
    enable me to attend to my responsibilities.

Colossians 3:2; 2 Corinthians 12:9

For an Understanding
Employer

Jesus,

In this season of arriving late or calling in,
I pray my employers would be like fountains
  overflowing with your grace and understanding.
May my employers be vessels
  of your limitless love and compassion.
May my employers' hearts be an extension of yours.
May your generosity reign in their hearts
  and may the earthly ways of conducting business
  be replaced with your ways, Lord.

_____

Matthew 20:1-16

For Financial Need

Generous Father,

Our expenses increase beyond our means;
    we don't know how we'll pay the bills.

Give us medical providers and insurance companies
    that extend grace and mercy.

Give us friends and strangers who are concerned for us,
    whose hearts overflow with generous care.

Give us a church that shares in our need,
    partnering with us in our hardship
    to help supply what we lack.

Give us contentment in every circumstance.
Teach us how to make do with little or with much.
Make us able to do all things through Christ
    who strengthens us,
knowing that you,
    who did not even spare your Son for us,
    will grant us everything in him,
    supplying all our needs
    according to your riches in glory in Jesus Christ.

To you, our God and Father, be glory forever and ever.
Amen.

———————

Philippians 4:10-20

To him who is able to do above and
beyond all that we ask or think according
to the power that works in us—to him be
glory in the church and in Christ Jesus
to all generations, forever and ever.

Ephesians 3:20-21

For Equipping to Care
for Our Child
(Based on Genesis 16:7-13; 21:14-19)

Lord, you are El Roi—
   the God who sees me,
   the God who equips me,
   the God who provides for all my needs,
   the God who provides for the needs of *my child*.

Like Hagar, I journey through a barren wasteland.
My soul is weary,
   and I am burdened.
When all hope looks lost
   and I have come to the end of myself
   and my physical resources,
I know I can cry out to you in my despair,
   and my cries will reach your ears.

I know the care of *my child* doesn't rest on me
   or my abilities,
but on the endless grace and mercy you pour out onto me.

Whether it's a well of life-giving water
   that appears at precisely the right moment,
   or a word that encourages my downcast soul,
the evidence of your sovereign hand on my life
   equips me to care for my child.

You are my Good Shepherd!
In you and through you,
    I lack nothing.
    I have more than enough.
    I have been called to parent my child.
    I am qualified to care for my child.

For Courage to Go Through
with a Pregnancy

Father,

I know I should give thanks for this pregnancy
    for children are always a blessing from you
    from the very moment of conception—
    but this pregnancy fills me with fear.

For those who don't feel ready for a baby
    The thought of this pregnancy overwhelms me.
    I'm not ready! I don't have the resources needed
        to receive and parent this new life.

    I am afraid, overwhelmed, and desperate.
        How will I do this, Lord?

For those whose last pregnancy ended in miscarriage
    I've known the agony of pregnancy loss—
        rejoicing to know I have a child,
        then grieving the loss of one I never knew.

    Facing this again is more than I can bear;
        the thought of it fills my days with worry.

For those whose last pregnancy ended in stillbirth
    I've journeyed through pregnancy,
        enduring labor and delivery,
        only to hold a dead child in my arms.

The memory of that loss overwhelms me
  and stifles all my rejoicing.

For a pregnancy with a difficult diagnosis
I am told that *my child* has this difficult diagnosis,
  which will bring suffering and hardship,
  the loss of dreams and an uncertain future.

Who can abide the thought of their child suffering?
  You are giving me more than I can bear.

For a pregnancy with a terminal diagnosis
I know that *my child* will not live long;
  apart from a miraculous work from you,
  he/she will be born and soon die.

The knowledge of what will be
  is now breaking my heart.

All
Father, give me courage for this pregnancy
  and all that follows.

Give me joy, even in uncertainty and darkness,
  believing that you are doing good.

Psalm 127:3; John 9:1-3

For Rest

Lord Jesus,

I am exhausted.
I keep striving and cannot stop.
Yet when I want to rest, sleep eludes me.

Lord, help me rest.
Remind me that sleep is a gift
    and that rest is part of your good design.

It is vain to get up early and stay up late,
    working hard to get what I need,
    for you give sleep to the one you love.

I come to you weary and burdened,
    believing that you will give me true rest.

I take your yoke upon me, seeking to learn from you,
    because you are lowly and humble in heart—
    in you alone I find rest for my soul,
    for your yoke is easy and your burden is light.

Amen.

Psalm 127:1-2; Matthew 11:28-30

For Strength

Father God,

We are exhausted
   mentally,
   physically,
   emotionally,
   spiritually.
We feel depleted.
Our hope wanes.

Lord, send your angels to strengthen us
   just as you did with your prophet Elijah.
As we collapse under the shade of a tree
   in this wilderness season,
   may your angels meet us there.
May they provide us with spiritual bread and water
   that will strengthen our souls
   and sustain us for the arduous journey ahead.

––––––––––

1 Kings 19:1-9

I will ask the Father, and he will give you
another Counselor to be with you forever.
He is the Spirit of truth.

John 14:16-17

For Support from Family and Friends

Father,

You said, "It is not good for the man to be alone,"
    and so you made a helper for him.

You never intended for me to be alone;
    you created me to flourish in community.

Your wisdom shows me that "two are better than one
    because they have a good reward for their efforts.
    For if either falls, his companion can lift him up;
    but pity the one who falls
    without another to lift him up."

I can't do this alone, Father. I need support.

Raise up friends to offer support—
    spiritually, emotionally, materially—
    and give me the grace to receive it.

I ask you because you are my helper;
    you are the sustainer of my life,
    the giver of every support.

———————————————

Genesis 2:18; Ecclesiastes 4:9-12

A Responsive Prayer:
Don't Worry

(Based on Luke 12:22-34; Matthew 7:7-11)

Leader

Jesus says,

I tell you, don't worry
  about your life, what you will eat;
  or about the body, what you will wear.
For life is more than food
  and the body more than clothing.

All

Lord, teach us to consider the ravens.
They don't sow or reap;
  they don't have a storeroom or barn;
  yet you feed them.

Aren't you worth much more than the birds?
Can any of you add one moment to his life span
  by worrying?
If then you're not able to do even a little thing,
  why worry about the rest?

Lord, remind us how the wildflowers grow:
  they don't labor or spin thread.
Yet not even Solomon in all his splendor
  was adorned like one of these.

If that's how God clothes the grass,
   which is in the field today
   and is thrown into the furnace tomorrow,
   how much more will he do for you?

Lord, teach us not to strive for things we need,
   and help us not to be anxious,
for our Father knows that we need them.

But seek his kingdom, and these things
   will be provided for you.

Lord, help us not to worry about tomorrow
   because tomorrow will worry about itself.
Each day has enough trouble of its own.

Ask, and it will be given to you.
   Seek, and you will find.
   Knock, and the door will be opened to you.
For everyone who asks receives,
   and the one who seeks finds
   and to the one who knocks, the door will be opened.

Lord, give us today our daily bread.

God will supply all your needs
   according to his riches in glory in Christ Jesus.

Lord, you are my shepherd;
   I have what I need.

Luke 12:22-34; Matthew 7:7-11; Philippians 4:19; Psalm 23

7

Prayers for Times of
Spiritual Darkness and Doubt

A Child's Prayer

God,

I know that you are good.
I know that you are mighty.

But sometimes I doubt you.
    I doubt that you see me.
    I doubt that you care for me.

Deep down, I know these thoughts aren't true.

I know you are with me.
I know you love me.
I know you want the best for me.

Lord, I believe;
    help my moments of doubt!

Amen.

_____

Mark 9:24

When We Don't Know What to Pray

Father,

We do not know what to pray for as we should.

But your Spirit prays for us with groaning beyond words
    to help us in our weakness.

You, who search our hearts,
    also know the Spirit's mind,
    for he prays for us according to your will.

And your Son who died and rose for us
    is also at your right hand, praying for us.

Father, hear our prayer; hear your Spirit; hear your Son.

Amen.

Romans 8:26-27, 34

When I Am Angry at God

Lord,

I'm angry with you.

You've interrupted my plans for my life, my family,
  and my child.
You haven't shown us any good reason for this suffering.
You've withheld comfort, health, and peace.

You haven't healed *my child*.

I want to go to war with you, to shout at you in rage.
  But only a fool's heart rages against the Lord.

Won't the Judge of the whole earth do what is right?

You poured out all the anger I deserve for my sins
  on Jesus when he died for me.

If you loved me and removed all your anger from me,
  shouldn't I love you and put away my anger at you?

Everyone who is enraged against you
  will come to you and be put to shame.

But everyone who believes in Jesus the crucified and risen
  will not be put to shame.

So, instead of accusing you, I will challenge myself.
  Why, my soul, are you so sad?
  Why are you in such turmoil?

Put your hope in God,
for I will still praise him,
my Savior and my God.

Forgive me, Father, for being angry, even in my suffering.
You've only been good to me.
You've never done me wrong.

Remove my anger, and replace it
with faith, hope, and love.

Genesis 18:24; Psalm 42:11; Proverbs 19:3; Isaiah 45:24;
Lamentations 3:39; Jonah 4:4

When I Am Anxious or Anguished

Lord Jesus,
I am in agony.

With each word I utter in prayer,
    anxieties overwhelm my mind.

I hold so tightly to the things of this world,
    to *my child*,
    to my hopes,
    to my dreams.
How can I loosen my grip and trust you
    with what is ahead,
especially when I don't know what that will look like?

Lord, surrendering
    my child
    my circumstances
    and my future
to your plans is weighty and hard.

But Jesus, I know you understand the struggle.
As you prayed through anguish
    in the Garden of Gethsemane,
    your sweat fell like blood to the ground beneath you.
    You wrestled with the weight of what was to come.
Angels came and ministered to you,
    strengthening you for the cross ahead.

I pray for the strengthening of my spirit, too.
I cannot journey through this suffering
    without the Holy Spirit's equipping.
Help me to die to myself and my desires.
Give me a heart fixed on eternity
    and on your bigger picture.

———

Luke 22:42

When I Want to Walk Away from God

God,

Right now, I want to walk away from you.
  I want to run a thousand miles away from you.

But where can I go to escape your Spirit?
  Where can I flee from your presence?

If I climb to heaven or sink into the grave, you're there.
If I travel to the east or to the west,
  you'll be there when I arrive.
If I think that darkness will hide me, you still see me.
You know everything I think, say, and do.

That is such good news!
  I couldn't leave you, even if I tried!

When I stray, you find me.
When I return, you throw a party.
You've penned me in with your love.

You proved at the cross that you love me
  and will never leave or forsake me.

Keep me in your love, Lord;
I can't keep myself.

Psalm 139:7-12; Luke 15:11-32

For Lamenting Our Circumstances
(Based on Psalm 102)

Listen to me, Lord, and don't hide your face!
  Listen to me, Lord, and answer me now!

Do you see what this suffering is doing to me?
  Do you see how Satan taunts me all day long?

My life is fading away like smoke in the wind.
  My body feels like it's on fire.
My heart is in so much pain I forget to eat.
  I groan so much, I'm only skin and bones.
Instead of food, I eat ashes and drink my tears.
  My life is withering away like grass.

But you reign forever, Lord! Your glory never ends!
In your time, you will rise and show mercy!
You will pay attention to the cry of the poor
  and will not despise my prayer,
  so that I will sing your praises to everyone!

Even if my strength disappears and my life is shortened,
  you never change, and your years do not end.
So I will find my life and my home in you,
  and you will keep me forever.

Being in anguish, [Jesus] prayed more
fervently, and his sweat became like drops
of blood falling to the ground.

Luke 22:44

When It All Feels Unfair

Lord,

It isn't supposed to be this way.
This kind of stuff isn't supposed to happen
   to people like me.

I am a good person with good intentions.
I believe in you and I make an effort to walk in your ways.
Is this how you treat those who love you?

What about the wicked?
   Those who deny you?
   Those who curse your name?
What about those who don't want children
   and those who don't steward them well?
Aren't they more deserving of circumstances like these?

My heart cries out to you in my spiritual darkness.
This is unfair;
   cruel, even.
This is hard;
   simply unbearable.
This is tragic;
   utterly heartbreaking.

I hold nothing back;
   what's the point when you know my thoughts
   before I speak them?

So, like Jacob,
I wrestle with the God of the universe.
I grapple to understand our circumstances.
    What did we do to deserve this?
    Why us?
    Why our child?
I struggle to get the upper hand.
    I try to take your place on the throne,
    giving you a list of all the reasons we don't deserve this,
    naively thinking I can convince you
    to change your plans.

And as I wrestle with you,
I hear your still, small voice.
You remind me that in this world I will have trouble.
    Struggle is everywhere.
    Suffering is inescapable.
But in it and through it,
    you remind me I can take heart because I have you—
    my conqueror and
    the Savior of the world.

Genesis 32:24-32; John 16:33

When Circumstances Look Bleak

God,

I am confused. Did I do something to deserve this?
I feel betrayed. How could you allow this?
I feel alone. Do you see me? Do you see *my child*?
I feel overlooked. Do you even care about us?
I feel hopeless. How can we make it
    with the odds stacked against us?

O my soul, choose to remember the Lord
    and his faithfulness.
Though Joseph was betrayed and sold into slavery,
    though he was falsely accused and imprisoned,
    you used each of Joseph's setbacks for a holy setup.

God, you took what the enemy meant for evil
    and turned it for good.
You appointed Joseph into power
    to save his family from death and famine.

Father, forgive my unbelief and my shortsightedness.
Give me eyes to see how you are working
    in my circumstances.
Give me a heart of courage to keep pressing on,
    knowing your goodness is coming.

———————

Genesis 37; 39 – 47

When I Don't Feel Strong Enough

Lord God, this burden is heavy.
Ignoring the pain, I will myself to walk forward.
With each labored step, my body slowly begins to give way
until I collapse in a heap of ruin, coming to the realization
   that I'm not equipped to carry this alone.

With head bowed, I open my hands.
   You, O God, give power to the weak.
   You give power to those who have no might.
Lord, my hands are open to receive your strength.

With head bowed, I inhale deeply.
   You, O God, renew the strength
   of those who wait on you.
Lord, still my soul to receive your renewing.

With head bowed, I exhale slowly.
   You, O God, place your children on the wings of eagles.
   There they do not grow weary; they do not faint.
Lord, place me upon your wing to receive your rest.

My circumstances are far too heavy for me—
   this I realize.
But they aren't too heavy for you, O God.

Isaiah 40:29-31

A Responsive Prayer: Listen to My Cry
(Based on Psalm 88)

Leader

Lord, God, you are my salvation!
I call out to you day and night.

All

Let my prayer reach your ears!
Listen to my cry!
My soul overflows with troubles;
    I am at death's doorway.
I am numbered among the dying,
    like one with no strength,
    thrown into the grave,
    cut off from you,
    forgotten by you.

You buried me in this pit, Lord,
    in the darkest place,
    in the depths.

Your wrath crushes me—
    wave upon wave engulfs me.
I'm imprisoned in a cage of sorrow
    with no way to escape.

My eyes are exhausted from crying.
Lord, I cry out to you all day long,
    stretching out my hands to you.

I continue to cry out to you for help, Lord!
  I know my prayer reaches your ears!
So why, Lord, are you rejecting me?
  Why are you hiding your face from me?

Look at me, Lord! I am in agony and close to death!
I suffer your terrors—desperate and distraught!

Your wrath sweeps over me; your terrors destroy me.
They are a flood that engulfs every part of me.

Lord, God, you are my salvation!
I call out to you day and night.
Let my prayer reach your ears!
Listen to my cry!

8

Prayers to Lift Our Eyes in Praise

A Child's Prayer

God,

Scripture says
 you are seated in heaven on your throne.
 This world is your footstool.

To imagine your feet resting on our planet is amazing!
To me, this world feels huge.
But to you, it must be small.

God, maker of heaven and earth
 and everything in them,
you are worthy of all glory and honor.
I praise you today, tomorrow, forever.

Amen.

———

Isaiah 66:1-2

I exalt you, my God the King,

and bless your name forever and ever.

I will bless you every day; I will praise your name

forever and ever.

Psalm 145:1-2

To Jesus, My Savior

I praise you, Jesus, the image of the invisible God,
    the firstborn over all creation.

I praise you, Jesus, because you made everything:
    everything in heaven and on earth,
    both the visible and the invisible,
    thrones, dominions, rulers, authorities—
    every created thing was made through you and for you!

I praise you, Jesus, because you are the head of the body:
    you are the beginning of the church
    because you are the first to rise from the dead—
    and, therefore, you will have first place in everything.

I praise you, Jesus, because you are the eternal,
    uncreated God:
you existed with God in the beginning
    because you were God!

I praise you, Jesus, because,
    even though you always existed as God,
    you became a human being and lived with us.

I praise you, Jesus, because you loved me
    and gave yourself for me—
instead of exploiting your divine nature to serve yourself,
    you volunteered to humble yourself in human nature,
    becoming a slave who was always obedient,
    even to the point of death on a cross.

I praise you, Jesus, because you carried
   my sickness and my sorrow.
You were pierced because of my rebellion.
You were crushed because of my sin.
You were punished to give me peace.
You were wounded for my healing.
You were raised from the dead
   to declare me righteous.

I praise you, Jesus, because God has highly exalted you,
   giving you a name that is greater than any other name,
   so that everyone everywhere will bow before you
   and confess that you are Lord and Christ
   to the glory of God the Father.

I praise you, Jesus!

Colossians 1:1-18; John 1:1-4, 14; Philippians 2:5-11; Isaiah 53:4-6

Praise for the Gift of My Child

Father,
sinful and imperfect as we are,
   we still give our children good gifts.
If our children ask for a loaf of bread,
   we give them bread, not stones.

You, O God,
   are sinless and perfect.
How much more will you,
   our heavenly Father,
   give your children good gifts.

Lord, I praise you for *my child*.
Surely *she/he* is a good and perfect gift
   that has come down to me from the Father of lights.
May I cherish the gift that is *my child*
   and may I steward my time with *her/him* well.

Matthew 7:11; James 1:17

To the God Who is an Ever-Present Help

God,
   who is like you?
Majestic in holiness,
   awesome in glorious deeds,
   doing wonders?

There is none like you, O God.

In my distress,
   time and time again,
I call to you, my heavenly Father.

I cry out for help
   in the seemingly unimportant things
   and in the big, important things too.
And though the stream of my pleas is steady,
   you never grow tired of my cries,
   you never complain of my neediness.

Instead,
   you are patient;
   you are compassionate;
   you are merciful;
   you are kind.

I am convinced that
   there is none like you, O God.

Jesus,
Immanuel,
God with me,
you are my ever-present help.
You are working on my behalf
    and for *my child*.
You are parting seas.
You are holding back waters.
You are moving mountains.
And you're doing it all for our good
    and for your glory.

You are worthy of all the glory,
    of all the honor,
    of all the praise.

Holy, holy, holy, is the Lord, God Almighty.
There is none like you, O God.

————————

Exodus 15:11

To the God Who Works for Our Good

(Based on Romans 8:18-39)

You work everything together for good,
for the good of me, your child,
because you called me
for your purpose.

With you as my father, I am in safe hands,
because you foreknew and predestined me
to be conformed to the image of your Son:
    you chose me in eternity past;
    you called me to yourself;
    you declared me righteous in Christ;
    you will glorify me in the resurrection.

What should I say about all this?

Who can be against me when you are for me?
    You didn't hold back your Son
    but gave him up for me,
    so you will always be on my side
    and give me everything with Jesus!

Who can bring an accusation against me?
    You have already declared me righteous!

Who can condemn me before you?
No one, because Jesus
    died for my sins,
    rose from the dead,

stands at your right hand,
and intercedes on my behalf.

Is there anyone or anything—
affliction or distress,
persecution or famine,
nakedness or danger,
sword or execution—
that can separate me from Christ's love?

No, I can more than conquer these things
through Jesus who loved me and who loves me!

I know beyond a shadow of a doubt that
neither death nor life,
nor angels nor rulers,
nor present things nor future things,
nor powers, nor height nor depth,
nor anything else in God's creation
can ever separate me from the love
that God, my Father, has for me
in Christ Jesus my Lord.

To the God Who Provides

God, I'm sure they never saw it coming.
Never in a million years did the Israelites imagine
    you would rain down bread from heaven.
But you're good—surprisingly good!

Lord, I can trust that right here and right now,
    though it may look impossible,
    though it may look like a long shot,
    you are not only able to provide for my needs,
    but you lovingly want to care for me and *my child*.
It isn't work for you. It isn't a burden.
You do it out of love and desire.

So whatever provision looks like,
    whether it's what I ask for or something else,
I prepare my heart for the unfathomable.
And I open my hands to receive.

Your unfailing love is as vast as the heavens;
    your faithfulness reaches beyond the clouds.
You are Jehovah Jireh, the God who provides,
    and you will provide for me.

Exodus 16:11-15; Psalm 36:5

To the God Who Is All-Knowing

You, O Lord, are the everlasting God,
  the Creator of all the earth—
  everything comes from You.

You who hold the oceans in your hand
  also hold me and *my child*
  in our current circumstances.

You who measured the heavens with your fingers
  also measured the very days
  we are walking through now.

You who know the weight of the earth
  and have weighed the mountains and hills on a scale
  also know the weight of this suffering.

No one is able to advise the Spirit of the Lord,
  for you do not need advice.
No one knows enough to counsel you or to teach you,
  for you do not need instruction about what is good.

God, in your hands *my child* and I know that we are safe.
  We know nothing is a surprise to you.
  We know that we can trust you to do good.

So Father, we surrender our desire to have all the answers.
Instead, we entrust our lives to you, the giver of life.

———
Isaiah 40

To the God Who Weeps with Me and Comforts Me

Jesus,

I lift my eyes in praise to you,
   the Savior who weeps with me
   and comforts all my afflictions.

You keep count of all my tossings
   and put my tears in a bottle.
You command us to weep with those who weep.
   Do you not do the same?

Jesus, you are the comfort God gives us in every affliction.

Give me more of yourself,
   more of your hope,
   more of your power,
   more of your promise,
   more of your endurance,
   more of your resurrection,
so that I might have more of your comfort
   and you might have more of my praise.

Psalm 56:8; 2 Corinthians 1:3-7

A Responsive Prayer:
Worthy Are You

Leader
Praise the Lord!

All
Praise the name of the Lord!

Praise the Lord, for the Lord is good!
Praise the Lord, for the Lord is beautiful!

We praise you, our God and King!
 We will praise your name forever!
The Lord is great and highly praised;
 his greatness is unsearchable.

The Lord is gracious and compassionate,
 slow to anger and abounding in faithful love.
The Lord is good to everyone;
 his compassion rests on all he has made.

All your creation will thank you, Lord!
All your people will praise you!
Is there anyone who will not worship you, Lord?
 For you alone are holy.

Lord God, the Almighty, King of the nations—
 your works are great and awesome;
 your ways are just and true.

Holy, holy, holy, Lord God, the Almighty,
  who was, who is, and who is to come!

Worthy are you, our Lord and God,
  to receive glory, honor, and power
  because you created everything
  and, by your will, all things exist.

Worthy are you, Jesus, the Lamb who lives forever,
  because you were slaughtered
  and you bought us with your blood
  so that we would be God's people.

You made us a kingdom of priests to our God,
  and we will reign with you on the earth forever!

Worthy is the Lamb who was slaughtered
  to receive power and wealth, wisdom and strength,
  honor and glory and blessing!

Give praise to the one who sits on the throne
  and to the Lamb who died and lives again—
  blessing and honor and glory and power
  forever and ever!

Amen!

Psalm 135:1-3; 145:1-10; Revelation 15:3; 4:8, 11; 5:9-14

Who can separate us from the love of Christ?
Can affliction or distress or persecution or
famine or nakedness or danger or sword? ...
No, in all these things we are more than
conquerers through him who loved us.

Romans 8:35, 37

9

Prayers for during Treatment

A Child's Prayer

God,

You are my rock.
   Unshakable.
   Strong.
   True.

My journey may be full of
   ups and downs
   and twists and turns
but I know I can count on you.

You are with me.
I have nothing to fear.

Amen.

Before a Doctor's Appointment

Father, help *my child* and I
   as we go to the doctor.

Help us to be grateful,
   remembering that medical care
   is a good and gracious gift.

Help us to be hopeful,
   trusting that you will use
   this visit to do us good.

Help us to be patient,
   knowing that you are working
   according to your plan.

Help me to be clear-headed,
   asking the right questions
   and understanding the answers.

Help *my child* to get better
   as you use the medical team
   to provide effective care.

Help us to worship you, our good Father,
   who gave your only Son to rescue us
   and to bring us home to your house forever.

Before Communicating News
to Family and Friends

Lord,

Sometimes, sharing updates feels like a burden.
My mind is spinning with new information.
My heart is still processing the news.
I feel too tired to find any words
    to share with others.
But they ask.

Help me remember that it is a rich blessing
    to have friends who are interested
    in my child's medical journey.
It means we are not alone;
    we are not unseen.

Show me when I should share an update
    and when I should ask a friend to do it.
Give me people who can help me
    know what I should say
    and how to say it.

Whether my own words or those of a helper,
help me communicate news in a way that is
    sensitive to my child's privacy,
    clear, helpful, accurate,
    and honoring to you.

When the news is favorable
  In this good news, help me celebrate
    what you have done for *my child*
    in a way that announces your goodness
    so that others might turn to you in need.

When the news is disappointing
  In this disappointing news, help me share
    my grief over sickness and setback
    through words and tears that are saturated
    with the hope I have in Jesus.

All
  In all my updates—good or bad—
    help me to clearly communicate
    that my hope and confidence
    are not in circumstances
    but in you, O Lord.

Before a Hospital Visit

God, you are Lord over all.
You are bigger than any giant *my child* and I face,
   including this hospital.

As Lord over all,
   you are Lord of our bodies
   and Lord over our minds.

Though the hospital might stir feelings of fear and anxiety,
   as the Creator of our bodies,
   you can tell them how to respond.

When our heartbeats quicken,
   you can slow them down.
When our chests tighten,
   you can release the tension.
When fear creeps in,
   you can command it to go.
When our minds go blank,
   you can give us the words.

As Lord over all,
   you are Lord over *my child*
   and Lord over *my child's* future.

Nothing passes through your hands
   without your permission.
Though I may not understand what is unfolding,
   I can trust you because you are a just and good God.

"I have told you these things so that in me you may have peace. You will have suffering in this world. Be courageous! I have conquered the world."

John 16:33

When Observing a Special Occasion in the Hospital

Jesus, it's hard to have a happy heart,
    to celebrate the right occasion
    in what feels like the wrong location.
But here we are,
    observing this special occasion in a hospital.

Instead of songs, there are beeping monitors.
Instead of presents, there are pills and prodding.
Instead of a special trip, there's another test.
Instead of a backyard, *my child* is in bed.
Instead of little friends, there are doctors and nurses.

Jesus, you know what it is like
when what should be happy times
happen in hardship and pain.
    Your first Christmas had only a manger.
    Your early birthdays happened in exile.
    Your final Passover brought you a cross.
    Your first Easter was met with unbelief.

Jesus, your life reminds us that, with you,
    circumstances are not controlling;
    location cannot thwart celebration.
For joy is not found in a place or a tradition,
    but in the goodness of the gift
    and the glory of the giver.

When Leaving My Child at the Hospital

Lord, there is nowhere we can go from your Spirit,
   nowhere we can flee from your presence.

This means that *my child* is not alone.
You are always with *him/her*.
You will not leave *my child's* side.

Father, fill me and *my child* with this truth
as we prepare for *him/her* to stay at the hospital
   so that every fear,
   every doubt,
   every ounce of shame
   will spill out of us and be replaced with your peace.

Remind me and *my child* that
   the best place we can be is in your hands—
and since you are everywhere all at once,
   my child is never out of your sight
   nor out of your reach.

——————

Psalm 139:7-12

When My Child is Readmitted
to the Hospital

God,

At the mere thought of being readmitted to the hospital,
we want to dig our heels into the ground.

Please, not again.
It's too hard.
It's too scary.
It's too painful.
We don't have it in us.

But I know you are faithful.
I know that you, who began a work in *my child*,
are faithful to complete it.

Fill *my child* and me with your peace.
Give us courage to walk through this,
and to trust in you no matter the circumstances.

———

Philippians 1:6

When We Have a Setback

Father,
I am hurt.
I am afraid.
I am confused.
I am disappointed.

For a little while, I had hope.
Things were looking better.
Treatments were working.
Doctors were encouraged.

Then this.

Another setback.

Why, O God? Answer me!
Why can't we live in a world where
    every doctor knows the right treatment,
    every diagnosis is entirely correct,
    every treatment is successful,
    every medicine is effective,
    every child gets better?

If you would answer, I would not understand,
    because your ways are too wonderful for me,
    they are beyond my comprehension.

So I will remember and rest in this:
the people loved your Son,
    and then they hated him.

The crowds followed your Son,
   and then they left him.
The world celebrated your Son,
   and then they murdered him.
Though such turns were setbacks in human eyes,
   they were not reversals in your plan,
   but the unseen and surprising way
   in which you would
   save your people and
   glorify your name.

I don't know what you are doing, Father.
But I know it is right and good.

I don't like this setback.
But I trust in you.

Father, glorify your name.

"Now my soul is troubled. What should I say—
Father, save me from this hour? But that is why I
came to this hour. Father, glorify your name."

John 12:27-28

For the Transition to Home

Father,

You have been with us during *my child's* time
   in the hospital.
You were so merciful while *she/he* was away from home.
And now, it is time for *my child* to go home.

As excited as we are about going home, Father,
   we know every transition brings challenges:
   the absence of professional caregivers,
   readjusting to life with our family,
   adjusting to different routines,
   unforeseen challenges.

But, Father, nothing about this is unforeseen by you.
You planned *my child's* time away from home,
and you planned *her/his* return.

Please make this transition comfortable,
   full of happiness and contentment.

But if returning home is difficult or uncomfortable,
remind us that this world is not our home—
   let our pleasures and our pains
   point us back to you, Father,
   and the home you are preparing for us.

A Responsive Prayer: Every Moment
(Based on Ecclesiastes 3:1-14)

Leader

There is an occasion for everything,
and a time for every activity under heaven.

All

A time to give birth and a time to die;
a time to plant and a time to uproot;
a time to kill and a time to heal;
a time to tear down and a time to build;
a time to weep and a time to laugh;
a time to mourn and a time to dance;
a time to throw stones and a time to gather stones;
a time to embrace and a time to avoid embracing;
a time to search and a time to count as lost;
a time to keep and a time to throw away;
a time to tear and a time to sew;
a time to be silent and a time to speak;
a time to love and a time to hate;
a time for war and a time for peace.

Lord, *our child's* medical journey brings many occasions.
Whether anticipated or unexpected,
    we know that each moment is planned by you.

Help us receive every moment as a gift from you—
a time to know you and to trust in you.

I am the LORD your God,

who holds your right hand,

who says to you, "Do not

fear, I will help you."

Isaiah 41:13

10

Prayers for Giving
Thanks after Recovery

A Child's Prayer

Lord,

I looked to you.
I cried out to you,
   Heal me, God! Please!

And today I can say,
You heard.
And you answered.

Thank you, God.
Amen.

————

Psalm 34:4

After a Complete Recovery

Jesus,
I thank you.
I thank you for healing *my child*,
   for sparing my child's life.

I thank you for how you have parted this sea
   and moved this mountain.
I praise you because as king of the world,
   nothing is impossible for you—
      you can overcome any disease,
      you can overcome any limitation.

Thank you for your healing hand
that has supernaturally cleansed *my child*
and wiped away all traces of illness and disease.

May I never forget this day
   and just how merciful and compassionate you are.
May your praise be on my lips forever more,
   and may I speak of your goodness and your faithfulness
   all the days of my life.

Amen.

———

Luke 1:37

After a Successful
Round of Treatment

You care about the ravens.
They don't plant, harvest, or store food, because
   you are faithful to feed them.

You care about the lilies.
They don't will themselves to grow
   or make their own clothing
because you are their provider.

And you also care about my child.

My child doesn't have to work
   to earn your favor or *his/her* healing,
   because you love *him/her*,
   simply because *he/she* is yours.

So Lord,
   I thank you for this successful round of treatment.
I realize it wasn't owed to *my child*.
But in your mercy,
   in your compassion,
   in your loving-kindness,
You have chosen to give it,
   and for that I am so grateful.

Luke 12:22-34

When Reaching a Milestone
after Treatment

Father,

We did not know if we would see this day.

Nothing in my power could have brought us here.

But now we are here, celebrating this milestone,
  because of your abundant kindness.

Let this day be a landmark on *my child's* journey—
  an unmovable, unforgettable reminder
  of your power and compassion—
so that we will never forget to trust you.

If I say, "My foot is slipping,"

your faithful love will support me,

LORD. When I am filled with cares,

your comfort brings me joy.

Psalm 94:18-19

Praise for Sustaining Us
throughout the Journey

Jesus, you are my shepherd;
I have what I need.

This journey took us by surprise,
giving us no opportunity
    to pack a bag or study a map;
    to gather provisions or learn necessary skills;
    to prepare our hearts and minds.
Such a traveler is bound to fail, overwhelmed.

Nevertheless, you have sustained me,
surprising me with everything I need
at every step of the journey—
    never leaving or forsaking me,
    teaching me through your Spirit,
    strengthening my faith with your word,
    sustaining my soul with your promises,
    supplying my needs from your glorious riches,
    guarding my heart and mind with your peace.

I do not know if there is more to this journey,
    but I do know this:
Only goodness and faithful love
    will pursue me all the days of my life,
    and I will dwell in your house as long as I live.

Psalm 23:1, 6; John 14:26; Psalm 94:19; Philippians 4:9, 19

Praise for Allowing Me More Life with My Child

Father,
    though this trial is not one I would have wished for,
    you have used it for your good and your glory.

Through *my child's* struggles
    you have taught me the fragility of life.

You have given me a heart of wisdom to number my days
    and to live each one with purpose and intention.

Thank you for the gift of more life with *my child.*

Help me to steward my time with *my child* well—
    to teach *her/him* about the one
        who preserved *her/his* life,
    to raise *her/him* up in the way *she/he* should go,
    and to help *her/him* become more like you.

May I glorify you as I parent this precious child
    whom you have given to me.

———

Psalm 90:12

A Responsive Prayer: Bless the Lord
(Based on Psalm 103:1-3; Jonah 2:2-9)

Leader
Bless the Lord, O my soul,
    and all that is within me, bless his holy name!
Bless the Lord, O my soul,
    and do not forget what he has done!

All
He forgives all your iniquities,
    and heals all your diseases.

I called to the Lord in my distress,
    and he answered me.
I cried out for help in my despair;
    you heard my voice!

When *my child* **became sick,**
    I was cast into the depths,
into the heart of the seas,
    and the flood overcame me.

Helplessness engulfed me;
    hopelessness overcame me.
Then you raised my life from the Pit,
    O Lord, my God!

When *my child* **was fading away,**
    I remembered the Lord who heals,

and my prayer came to you
in your holy temple.

I sought the Lord who heals, and he answered me
    and rescued me from all my fears.
I cried out to the Lord, and he heard me
    and saved me from all my troubles.

You have healed *my child*, **O Lord!**
You have healed *my child*!
So I return to glorify you with a loud voice,
    to fall at your feet in thanksgiving.

Those who cling to worthless idols
    forsake their hope of mercy.

But everyone who believes in you
    will not be put to shame.

Psalm 34:4, 6; Exodus 15:26; Luke 17:11-19

11

Prayers for Times of Loss

A Child's Prayer

Dear God,

My family is sad.

My family is angry.

One minute *my sibling* was here,
　　and now *he/she* is not.

We don't understand.

We are confused.

Be close to us, Jesus.

Our hearts are broken.

Amen.

After Receiving a Terminal Diagnosis

Father, as you knit *my child* together in the womb,
    you determined the number of hairs on *her/his* head,
    you selected the dreams you placed in *her/his* heart,
    and you anointed *her/him* for *her/his* purpose.

I know that you have also numbered *my child's* days.
Though I desperately want *my child* to outlive me,
    I acknowledge that I do not have that say.
You, and you alone, are God.

But Lord, I ask this of you:
    just as you walked with Mary
    through the suffering of her son Jesus,
    walk me through this too.

Just as Simon of Cyrene carried the cross with Jesus,
    carry the weight of *my child's* terminal diagnosis with me.
For like Mary, both the words and the reality
    of what is to come for *my child*
    are like a sword that pierces my very soul.

Be near to me, O God,
    for my spirit feels crushed and pressed on every side.

Help me to trust in you, Lord.

————————

Luke 2:35; 23:26

For Lamenting the Death of a Child

Lord, King David was a man after your own heart,
   and he agonized over the death of a child:
      "My child! My child! If only I had died
      instead of you, my child, my child!"

My God, my God, why have you abandoned me?
   Why are you so far from my words of groaning?
My God, I cry out day and night, but you do not answer.
   But you are holy,
   enthroned on the praises of your people.

It was you who brought me out of the womb,
   making me secure at my mother's breast.
Why, then, have you taken *my child* from my arms,
   leaving me only trouble and no one to help?

Wake up, Lord! Why are you sleeping?
   Get up! Don't reject me forever!
Why do you hide
   and forget my affliction and oppression?
For I have sunk down to the dust;
   my body clings to the ground.

Rise up! Help me!
Redeem me because of your faithful love.

---

2 Samuel 18:33; Psalm 22:1-3, 9; 44:23-26

For Faith in the Face of Death

Jehovah Rohi, God My Shepherd,
   I cling to the promises found in your word.

Though I walk through the valley of the shadow of death,
   I will fear no evil, for you are with me;
   your rod and your staff, they comfort me.
You faithfully guide me through the valley,
   so close I can almost feel your breath as you whisper,
   "This is the way, walk in it."

Father, I thank you that through faith in you,
   we don't have to fear death.
Though death is near,
   what *my child* and I walk through right now
   is but its shadow.
This valley of the shadow of death
   is not death in its fullness
because, Jesus, on the cross you defeated death.
You opened up the possibility for eternal life with you.
And I know the suffering of this valley is nothing
   compared to the glory to be revealed.

So by faith and in faith,
   I fix my eyes on what cannot be seen
   and on the things that will last forever.
Jesus, I fix my eyes on you.

Psalm 23:4; 2 Corinthians 4

After a Pregnancy Loss

No place on earth should be safer
   than a mother's womb.
But now I know that even the womb
   cannot escape the cold hand of death.

Comfort me, Lord, with a place
   safer than a mother's womb—
   your blessed presence!

You sustained me from before my birth,
   carrying me along since birth.
You will be the same until my old age;
   you will bear me up when I turn gray.
You made me, and you will carry me;
   you will bear and rescue me.

Teach me to rest in your promise,
   for to be yours in Christ
   is to be in safe hands.

───────

Isaiah 46:1-4

After a Stillbirth

Lord, for months *my child* was carried in the womb.
   I have lovingly conversed with *my child*.
   I have affectionately stroked *my child*.
   I have felt the delight of *his/her* twists and turns.

And now, the moments I have dreamed of,
   hearing *my child's* first cry,
   holding *him/her* in my arms,
   seeing *him/her* face to face,
are met with silence.

Lord, nothing could have prepared me for this.
My soul aches knowing that *my child*,
   fearfully and wonderfully made,
   loved beyond measure,
   has passed away in the womb,
   before I could meet *him/her*.

Father, speak to me.
   Let your word be an anchor
   so the grief doesn't sweep me away.
   Meet me in this valley.
   Though my heart is broken, let it still trust in you.

———

Job 13:15

Jesus wept. So the Jews said,

"See how he loved him!"

John 11:35-36

When Holding Our Child's Body

Father,

I need you.
I need you to hold me together
  because right now my heart is in a million pieces
  and I'm unsure how I'll make it another moment,
  let alone a lifetime.

Merciful Savior,
  give me a vision of you
  holding my precious child in your arms.

Allow my mind to see a glimpse of *my child* fully alive.

Let this vision be a healing balm—
  a balm that comforts my grieving heart,
  a balm that spurs me on in hope.

O Lord, have mercy!

————————————

2 Corinthians 5:8

When Packing Up Our Child's Room

We filled this room with good things.
It was a place for laughter and play,
    for singing, safety, and rest.

O Lord! Why would you let us prepare
    our hearts, our lives, our house
    only for them now to be unoccupied?

This bed is not soft enough
    to soothe a broken heart.
There is no lullaby
    but our lament.
This grief is a shadow
    that no nightlight can chase away.

Is it true, Lord, that you are preparing
    a place for us in your house?
Is it true, Lord, that this suffering is nothing
    compared to the glory that awaits us?

We believe. Help our unbelief.

Mark 9:24; John 14:1-3; Romans 8:18

Before Announcing Our Child's Death

Lord, the time has come
to speak these words:
"*My child* has died."

Please grant every gift needed
to announce this heartbreak
in a way that points others
to the certain hope
found in Christ.

Before a Funeral

Merciful and faithful Jesus,

I never imagined that being a parent
would involve the funeral of my child.

How am I to look upon the lifeless body
of *my child*, whom I loved with all my soul?

How am I to walk away from a grave
knowing my child will not follow me home?

Jesus, you are no stranger to funerals.
You grieved openly at Lazarus's funeral,
weeping bitterly at his tomb.

So you can sympathize with me
and help me mourn today.

Give me mercy and grace today
to feel and express every emotion
in a way that shows all who attend
the tragedy of death,
the hope of the gospel,
and the faithfulness of my Savior.

John 11:1-44; Hebrews 2:14-18; 4:14-16

A Responsive Prayer: Teach Us, Father

Leader
Heavenly Father,

No one who lives in this broken-down world
    should be surprised by loss.

All
But, Father, we could not imagine the pain of this loss:
    the loss of dreams;
    the loss of milestones;
    the loss of experiences;
    the loss of hugs and kisses;
    the loss of laughter and tears;
    the loss of family trips;
    the loss of birthdays;
    the loss of wonder;
    the loss of *our child*.

Oh, Father, it is not hard to hate life in this world,
    now that we have tasted the bitterness of death
    and felt the sting of the curse!

We hate life in this broken-down world,
    longing for the world to come,
    hungry for eternal life.

Help us, Father, to know what it means
    to suffer this loss for Jesus' sake.

Teach us, Father, to bear this cross
    for the glory of your name.

Help us suffer this loss and every other
    by considering Christ to be our gain,
    being found righteous in him by faith.

Teach us, Father, to know Christ
    and the power of his resurrection
    and the fellowship of his sufferings,
    being conformed to his death
    so that we may attain
    the resurrection from the dead.

Luke 14:25-26; Matthew 10:39; 16:25; Philippians 3:7-11

12

Prayers for Life after a Loss

A Child's Prayer

Dear God,

So much changed when my sibling died.
Life looks so different now.
There is sadness,
   emptiness,
   confusion,
   and anger.

Your word says you work all things together for good.
Lord, I'm asking for that right now.
You are by our side, even in the hardest things.
   So when we're sad, help us!
   When we're empty, help us!
   Each and every day, help us!

Amen.

Romans 8:28

When Visiting a Grave

As I visit this grave, I remember
　　the good gift of *my child's* life,
　　the brokenness of this world,
　　the promise of resurrection.

Help us, Lord, to respond with
　　thankfulness for what you gave,
　　sorrow for what you took away,
　　and faith in what you promise.

I look forward to the day
I will dance on my empty grave
　　because you once left the tomb empty
　　and are returning to destroy death forever!

Come soon, Jesus,
　　and make all things new!

---

1 Corinthians 15:54-56; Revelation 21:5

On a Missed Milestone

God, I'm struggling.
Today marks a milestone.
If *my child* were here we would be celebrating,
but instead I am grieving *her/his* absence.

On my child's birthday
  Lord, let *my child's* birthday remind me
    that *she/he* is a precious gift you entrusted to me.
  I realize now that some gifts we enjoy for a lifetime,
    while others are fleeting.

  On this special day, I ask you to bestow upon me
    the gift of perspective.
  Remind me of the precious moments
    spent with *my child*.
  Create in me a heart of gratitude
    as I count my blessings.

When celebrating a holiday
  I pray for strength to make it through this day,
    a day set aside for celebrating and rejoicing together.
  It's hard for me to be festive when my heart is sorrowful,
    wishing *my child* could be here with us.

  May your grace be sufficient not only for me
    but for others too.
  May they be patient and understanding with me
    when I'm unable to celebrate in the ways
    they might expect.

On Mother's Day or Father's Day
  I pray for my heart today
    and ask that you be gentle with it.
  Be near and mend the broken pieces.
    Don't let my heart grow bitter, envious, or closed off.

  Remind me that my identity is not in being a parent,
    but in being your child.
  What a gift it is to be a child of God!
  For with this inheritance comes the promise
    of eternity with you
    and with all of your children.

At the start of a new school year or on a graduation day
  Just as today would mark the beginning
    of a new chapter for *my child*,
  may it also mark in me another layer of healing
    in my journey with loss.
  May the grief be lighter this year than the last.
  May I navigate the waves of sorrow
    with grace and fluidity
    as each day brings me one day closer to reunion.

All
  God, today and every day I ask you to
    help me talk about *my child*,
    to keep *her/his* memory alive,
    and to honor *her/his* life.

For Facing a New Normal

Lord, my child died.
That will never change.

I cannot go back
    to what life was before.

I cannot "get through this,"
    but I can move on "with this."

So, help me to move forward in faith,
    trusting you to show me how to live
    in a reality that I did not choose
    but in which I can trust you.

Teach me, Jesus, to live again
    until the day I live again with you.

For Finding Gratitude

Abba, Father,
  though you slay me,
  yet I will trust you.

I will trust in you because you, and you alone, give.
Every good and perfect gift comes from you
  and the storehouses of heaven—
  including my precious child.

Though you also take away,
  you don't take away what is mine,
  but only what is yours
  and what has always been yours—
  including my precious child.

I thank you for the creation of *my child*,
  for the life lived by *my child*,
and yes, I even thank you for the grief and the loss
  that has come with *my child*.

Because through it all,
  on the mountain tops and in the valleys,
  in the joy and in the pain,
you and your character have remained the same–
  yesterday, today, and tomorrow.
You are faithful now, and faithful you will be—
  and for that I am grateful.

———

Job 13:15

For Finding Peace

Jesus,
   in the waves of my grief,
I think of the time when a violent storm
   raged around you,
   and you slept soundly in the boat.

Though the waves tossed the boat about,
   though water spilled in and began to fill the hull,
   though the disciples panicked with shrieks and shouts,
Jesus, you slept soundly.

You slept soundly because you were filled
   with God's peace.
You didn't have to worry about that moment,
   that day, or the next.
You knew with steadfast confidence that the Lord
   would care for you, his beloved Son.

Lord, fill me with that same peace.
Drape me in it,
clothe me with it.

May your supernatural peace,
which surpasses all understanding,
keep me firm, rooted, and established,
even in the unpredictable seas of grief.

Matthew 8:23-27; Philippians 4:7

And the peace of God,

which surpasses all understanding,

will guard your hearts and minds in Christ Jesus.

Philippians 4:7

A Declaration of Faith amid Grief

Though my child's bed is vacant
   and a seat at the table is empty,
   little outfits go unworn
   and toys are left unused,
   lullabies are not sung
   and footsteps are silent,
yet I will celebrate in the Lord;
   I will rejoice in the God of my salvation!
The Lord, my Lord, is my strength;
   he makes my feet like those of a deer
   and enables me to walk on mountain heights!

_____

Habakkuk 3:17-19

A Declaration That a Little Life Has Great Value

My child had
a small body,
a short life.

In a world that worships
   strength and success,
   longevity and health,
it is easy to question
   if my child mattered.

Yet you've shown me, Father,
   that a person's significance
   is not to be measured
   by the world's metric.

My child is valuable
   because you made *him/her*
   in your image and likeness.

Give me wisdom, faith, and courage
   to show the world your worth
   in how I remember
   and celebrate *my child*.

Genesis 1:26-27

When I'm Hurt by Others' Words

Father,
    help me to forgive them,
    for they know not what they're doing.

I want to believe the best of them
    and think that they mean well,
but Lord, they seem so unaware that
    their words cut like a sword,
    their actions feel callous and insensitive,
    and their requests are just asking too much of me
    at this stage in my grief.

God, I humbly ask you to help me to forgive them
    as you have forgiven me.
Help me to extend to them unmerited grace
    as you have extended it to me.

And Father, I ask that you use me as salt and light.
Give me the words to speak truth in love
    so that these people can more effectively mourn
    with those who mourn.

Luke 23:34; Colossians 3:13; Romans 12:15

When Reintegrating into
Our Community

Lord, I know there is a time and a season for everything.
You have given me a time to be alone with you
    in my grief,
but you're also calling me back into a community
to experience the fullness you designed
    for human relationships.
Your heart for me is to find fellowship among believers,
    to break bread with them with glad and sincere hearts,
    and to pray and praise with my brothers and sisters.

Father,
I pray that as you send me out again,
    and as I reintegrate into my social circles,
    that as the Good Shepherd of my soul
    you would give me everything I need.

Clothe me in
    your tenderhearted mercy,
    your loving kindness,
    your holy humility,
    your precious tenderness,
    and in your perfect patience.

May your Holy Spirit not only sustain me
    but shine through me.

Ecclesiastes 3:4; Acts 2:42-47; Colossians 3:12

For Courage to Try to Conceive Again

Heavenly Father,

You know my heart fully and completely
   because you made it.
You placed every desire within it.

Lord, lead me in the path you have for me.

If I am to try to conceive again,
   confirm it and make it known to me.
If having another child is not in your plan for me,
   I ask that you let me down gently.
Remove the desire from my heart
   and replace it with your peace.

Like Jesus in the Garden of Gethsemane,
   may my heart cry, "Not my will, but your will, Lord."
And as my Sovereign Lord and Savior,
   may I rest assured that whatever your plan is for me—
   to conceive again or not—
   your plan is good.

Luke 22:42

For Weeping with Those Who Weep

Lord Jesus, even as you went to the cross,
   even as you endured pain and agony,
   you saw the suffering of others,
   you shared in their grief,
   and served them.

Even as I grieve my own loss, Lord,
   soften my heart to the grief of others
   and give me tears to weep with them.

Luke 23:27-31; John 19:25-27; Romans 12:15

For Rejoicing with Those Who Rejoice

What a confusing world to live in!
A single day is simultaneously
   one person's worst day
   and another's best.

While one weeps, another celebrates.

Help me to love my neighbor as myself,
   entering into their joy the same way
   I desire for them to enter my grief,
   for such is the heart of the Savior
   who both mourns and rejoices with us.

Romans 12:15; 1 Corinthians 12:26

A Responsive Prayer: His Faithful Love
(Based on Psalm 118)

Leader
Give thanks to the Lord, for he is good!

All
His faithful love endures forever.

In days of health and wholeness,
His faithful love endures forever.

In days of sickness and death,
His faithful love endures forever.

Death surrounded us and overtook *our child*;
but our faith in Jesus Christ is our victory
and we shall look in triumph on the grave.

His faithful love endures forever.

It is better to take refuge in the Lord
than to trust in humanity or medicine.

His faithful love endures forever.

Death and the devil tempt us to despair,
urging us to curse God and die.

**But we will not despair—
His faithful love endures forever.**

The Lord Jesus Christ died for our sins and was buried.
Then he rose from the grave, conquering death forever.
So though we live out our days in the pain of loss
    we will not grieve like those without hope.

The Lord is our strength and our song;
    he has become our salvation.
His faithful love endures forever.

Lord, save us! Lord, please grant us grace
    to live this life after loss
in faith and full assurance that
    when Jesus returns, we will live a life after resurrection.

You are our God, and we will give you thanks.
You are our God; we will exalt you.

Give thanks to the Lord, for he is good!
His faithful love endures forever.

He who testifies about these things

says, "Yes, I am coming soon."

Amen! Come, Lord Jesus!

Revelation 22:20

For further reading and helpful resources, please visit prayingthroughministries.org/resources.

Acknowledgments

Dear reader, if this book has blessed you, please know it is not our work alone. It came about through the support of a brilliant team of people. We hope you'll join us in giving thanks to God for the following people.

Eric:

Father, Son, and Holy Spirit: What a wonderful God you are, not only to make and redeem us but to comfort us in every affliction. May you use this little book to comfort many people with the hope of resurrection through Jesus Christ, our Lord.

Jenny and family: Jenny, thanks for supporting and encouraging me in learning from our sufferings so that we might comfort others in theirs. Kids, thanks for being incredible children. I love you.

Jessika Sanders: Thank you for your unwavering devotion to praying for suffering people and helping them seek God's face in the worst moments of their lives. I'm so grateful you reached out to support *Ours* and for the partnership God brought together in this book.

Katy Morgan: You are an incredible editor, equal parts encouraging and challenging, understanding what the author is trying to say, and somehow always knowing how to help them say it better. Thanks for your faithful service behind the scenes to make books better.

The Good Book Company: With *Ours: Biblical Comfort for Men Grieving Miscarriage*, you took a chance in publishing a niche book to serve an oft-overlooked audience. Once again, you've made a unique project possible for another niche audience. Thanks for being willing to publish these little books full of big comforts for people in hard places.

Brad and Emily: Thanks for lending your name and story to this project. The way you serve others never fails to bless me.

Jessika:

God, first and foremost, I thank you. Thank you for doing in my life exceedingly and abundantly more than I could ever imagine. Thank you for always working things together for your good and your glory. I'm in awe of you, Lord.

I'd like to thank my co-author, Eric Schumacher. Thank you for accepting a message request from a complete stranger and then presenting me with the incredible opportunity of co-writing this book with you. I will forever be in awe of the way *In His Hands* came about. I'm grateful to call you a friend and a brother in Christ.

Thank you to The Good Book Company for allowing us the opportunity to write a much-needed book for a very specific audience. Thank you to our editor, Katy, whose knowledge and foresight helped this book to come together so beautifully.

I'd also like to thank my family: my husband, Stephen, and my children, Eda, Esma, and Ezra.

Stephen, you are my greatest encourager. Thank you for encouraging me to pursue my dreams. Thank you to my children for sharing me with the people that would one day read this book and thank you for celebrating all my little writing-wins along the way.

Thank you to my friend, spiritual mentor, and co-laborer, Sarah. Thank you for your godly influence in my life and for entrusting me with leadership and pastoral opportunities at Deep Creek Community Church. It's an honor to serve the kingdom alongside you and call you a friend and sister in Christ.

Thank you to all my writer friends who encouraged me in the years leading up to this book, especially Tabitha, Amber, Jenn, and Liz. Thank you to each reader who shared my pieces and commented on them—you encourage me to keep writing.

thegood**book**

C O M P A N Y

BIBLICAL | RELEVANT | ACCESSIBLE

At The Good Book Company, we are dedicated to helping Christians and local churches grow. We believe that God's growth process always starts with hearing clearly what he has said to us through his timeless word—the Bible.

Ever since we opened our doors in 1991, we have been striving to produce Bible-based resources that bring glory to God. We have grown to become an international provider of user-friendly resources to the Christian community, with believers of all backgrounds and denominations using our books, Bible studies, devotionals, evangelistic resources, and DVD-based courses.

We want to equip ordinary Christians to live for Christ day by day, and churches to grow in their knowledge of God, their love for one another, and the effectiveness of their outreach.

Call us for a discussion of your needs or visit one of our local websites for more information on the resources and services we provide.

Your friends at The Good Book Company

thegoodbook.com | thegoodbook.co.uk
thegoodbook.com.au | thegoodbook.co.nz
thegoodbook.co.in